DEZIR QUE FIZO
JUAN ALFONSO DE BAENA

DEZIR QUE FIZO
JUAN ALFONSO DE BAENA

Introducción y edición de
NANCY F. MARINO

3

ALBATROS *ediciones*
HISPANOFILA

ALBATROS *ediciones*
HISPANOFILA

DIRECTORES DE LA COLECCIÓN

ALVA V. EBERSOLE y VICENTE SOLER

1. PEDRO CIRUELO: *Reprouación de las Supersticiones y Hechizerias*. Introducción y edición de Alva V. Ebersole.

2. *Cancionero de Obras de Burlas provocantes a risa*. Introducción y edición de Frank Domínguez.

3. *Dezir que fizo Juan Alonso de Baena*. Introducción y edición de Nancy F. Marino.

IMPRESO EN ESPAÑA

PRINTED IN SPAIN

I.S.B.N.: 84-7274-035-8

DEPÓSITO LEGAL: V. 2.243 - 1978

ARTES GRÁFICAS SOLER, S. A. - JÁVEA, 28 - VALENCIA (8) - 1978

CONTENTS

INTRODUCTION

O F the various Spanish *cancioneros* of the fifteenth century, the most important for the study of court poetry of that era is surely the *Cancionero de Baena*. Its importance is due not only to the great variety of poets represented in its 576 poems (the metrical works of sixty-four, including ten anonymous troubadors, appear), but should be attributed in great part to the skill and organization of the collection's compiler, Juan Alfonso de Baena. Since the epigraphs that introduce the poems contain a wealth of information about such aspects of the works as theme, circumstance and place of composition, style, and critical judgement of the poet's skill, Baena's contribution to our knowledge of "el arte de la gaya çiençia" has been immeasurable. But besides including and judging his contemporaries' poetic production, Baena also added eighty-one of his own compositions, which represent the majority of his known poems. Two of his works, however, do not appear in the collection which bears his name. One is found in the *Cancionero General* and deals with a dispute between Juan Marmolejo and Juan Agraz. Perhaps Baena decided not to include this composition in his *cancionero* since its subject matter did not coincide with his design; or perhaps it was written after 1445, the approximate date of compilation of this *Cancionero de Baena*. The other composition not contained in this collection is a lengthy treatise dedicated to the king, Juan II, which, as will be shown later on, was definitely composed before 1445. Although it appears to be Baena's most accomplished and important work, it is also his least known.

A rather incomplete, mutilated edition of Baena's long poem appears on folios 113r-113v and 131v of the unpublished *Cancionero de Palacio*, MS. 593,[1] and bears this epigraph: "Desir que envio Juan De Baena al Señor

---

[1] The *Cancionero de Palacio*, MS. 593 is an unpublished collection which is now found in the library of the University of Salamanca. It was described by Aaron Wittstein in his article, "An Unedited Spanish *Cancionero*," *Revue Hispanique*, 16 (1907), 295-333.

Rey sobre las discordias por que manera podian ser remediadas." The 1748-line composition is found in its entirety in another unpublished collection, the *Cancionero de San Román.* Sig. 2-7-2, MS. 2, of the library of the Real Academia de la Historia in Madrid. [2] The poem appears on folios 5r-15v of this *cancionero,* which are numerals of the latest system of foliation. But another, older system of Roman numerals shows folios xxxiii r-xliii v as the location of Baena's composition. These Roman numerals become important in a controversy over the actual, and perhaps original, length of the poem. In his *Historia de la literatura española,* José Amador de los Ríos briefly describes this work's structure: "Contiénese en el *Cancionero de Gallardo* [San Román]..., fols. 33 y siguientes, constando de doscientas cuarenta octavillas octosílabas, que con el epigrafe y la *finida* componen 1927 versos." [3] Examination of the manuscript reveals that from the beginning of the poem on xxxiii r (5r) to the *finida* on xliii v (15v), the folios are indeed numbered consecutively, and there is no evidence of *lacunae* which could account for another 178 verses. Furthermore, the number of *octavillas* is actually 218, plus a two-line dedication and a five-line *finida.* There are three missing lines, however: in stanza 47, the two last lines are omitted; in stanza 140, the fifth verse does not appear. The actual number of lines which are found in the manuscript is 1748, not Amador's count of 1927. His tabulation would not even account for the three omitted lines of poetry. Azáceta poses the question of possible loss of folios, [4] which an examination of the foliation suggests is probably not the answer to the problem. He also reluctantly wonders whether Amador de los Ríos could have been mistaken, for the poem's content does show evidence of continuity from beginning to end. Whatever the explanation, some of Amador's observations are indeed curious. For example, he quotes two stanzas and numbers them 110 and 111, [5] when they are actually 116th and 117th in the manuscript. Then but half-way through the poem, six *octavillas* must be accounted for as appearing in the manuscript, and not in Amador's edition. One would certainly expect the opposite to be the case. Even more interesting is the fact that Amador cites as "Octavas 222 and 223" [6] what appear in the *cancionero* as 213 and a combination of 214 and

---

[2] This *cancionero* was described by José María Azáceta y García de Albéniz, "El *Cancionero de Gallardo* de la Real Academia de la Historia," *Revista de Literatura,* 6 (1954), 239-270; 7 (1955), 134-180; 8 (1955), 271-282.

[3] José Amador de los Ríos, *Historia crítica de la literatura española,* VI (Madrid: José Fernández Cancela, 1865), p. 147, note 2.

[4] José María Azáceta, editor, *Cancionero de Juan Alfonso de Baena,* I (Madrid: Consejo Superior de Investigaciones Científicas, 1966), p. xii.

[5] Amador de los Ríos, *Historia,* VI, p. 149, note 1.

[6] *Ibid.,* p. 150, note 1.

215. That is to say, Amador de los Ríos has taken the first four lines of the 214th stanza of the manuscript (omitting completely the last four), and has combined them with the 215th stanza in its entirety, to form an *"octava"* of twelve lines. Besides this obvious impossibility, only nine "missing" stanzas would have to be accounted for from the beginning of the composition to near the end (where the *octavillas* just discussed appear in the manuscript) instead of the twenty-two stanzas suggested by Amador de los Ríos count of 240 stanzas. This would mean that between the 215th *octava* (Amador's twelve-line stanza numbered 223) and the *finida*, there should be, according to Amador's system, seventeen strophes. There are but three in the manuscript, for the 218th is the last before the *finida*. If at the point in question, (our 213, his 222) there is a difference of but nine stanzas, and since his final count is 240 and ours 218, there should be eleven "missing" *octavas* to account for the difference in the two tabulations. But, as already has been shown, Amador de los Ríos would need seventeen more stanzas beyond this point to complete his 240, and since there are actually three contained in the manuscript, there would have to be a difference of fourteen *octavas*, not eleven. This evidence would then render his count improbable.

Baena's lengthy composition has been published before, both in its entirety and in part. Part of it appeared, for what seems to be the first time, in the bibliographical notes of the 1851 edition of the *Cancionero de Baena*. [7] This is but a six-stanza fragment of the poem, taken from folio 131v of the *Cancionero de Palacio*, MS. 593. Later, in 1891, Menéndez Pelayo [8] published an incomplete edition of the work. However, besides omitting a number of complete stanzas and several lines of others, he also alters the text by changing the spelling of a number of words, and even adding words that do not appear at all in the manuscript of the *Cancionero de San Román*, upon which he based his edition. The composition does not appear in its entirely until 1958, when Jules Piccus published a paleographic edition in the *Nueva Revista de Filología Hispánica*. [9] Aside from being a very reliable source of the text of the poem, since he offers it with only the addition of stanza numbers and resolved abbreviations, Piccus has pointed out each of Menéndez Pelayo's omissions, additions, alterations, and errors in reading. Baena's composition does not appear in edited form until 1966, when Azáceta included it as an

[7] *Cancionero de Juan Alfonso de Baena* (Madrid: La Publicidad, 1851), p. 640.

[8] Marcelino Menéndez Pelayo, *Antología de poetas líricos castellanos*, II (Madrid: 1891), pp. 215-262.

[9] Jules Piccus, "The *dezir* of Juan Alfonso de Baena," *Nueva Revista de Filología Hispánica*, 12 (1958), 335-356.

appendix to his three-volume edition of the *Cancionero de Baena* and also described it in the introduction to the collection. [10] His critical edition and introduction, however, do not resolve all the problems surrounding the *dezir*, for Baena has included many historical and mythological references, some quite obscure, which by virtue of his allusion to them, deserve to be explained. There are also a number of difficult passages, which will be explained by translation. Besides the problems with the wording of the composition, its intention, structure, meaning, and relationship to other similar works of the time will be discussed.

Although it would be difficult to determine the precise date of its composition, there are a few clues within the long *dezir* which help approximate the year. For example, Baena mentions the Infantes Enrique and Juan, sons of Fernando I of Aragon, the monarch who had custody of King Juan II when the Castilian regent was a child. After Fernando died in 1416, his sons attempted to gain power in Castile. The struggle lasted through the 1420's and was over in 1431 or 1432. Since Baena speaks of these Infantes in a manner that suggests their defeat in this attempt at power, it can be assumed that he wrote the poem in at least 1432. The passage which identifies the Infantes as overcome is the following:

> Pues, Señor, quien bien acata
> los Infantes que padesçen,
> como quier que se basteçen
> Fortuna los desbarata,
> son corridos fasta mata
> de ser dentro en Alburquerque,
> ... ... (160)

Another point of evidence appears in stanza 162, line f, where Baena mentions "el Infante don Duarte." The reference is, of course, to Duarte of Portugal, who became king in 1433 and died five years later. The fact that Baena refers to this nobleman as "infante" strongly suggests that Duarte was not yet king at the time the poem was written. This, in turn, would mean that the *dezir* was composed during the first three years of the third decade of the fifteenth century. Then Menéndez Pelayo's estimate of 1443 [11] is at least ten years too late, and the mentioned don Duarte was already dead at that time. Azáceta is conservative in determining the date of composition

---

[10] Azáceta, *Cancionero de Baena*. The edition of the poem appears on page 1159 of Volume III; the discussion of the poem on pages x-xvi of Volume I.

[11] Menéndez Pelayo, *Antología*, I, p. 415.

between 1432 and 1440,[12] and Amador de los Ríos is probably correct in choosing 1433.[13]

The lengthy poem is a well-structured composition. It can be divided into eight somewhat parallel parts: the first section, the dedication, consists of two introductory lines and the first twelve stanzas; in the second part, Baena recounts his knowledge through books concerning historical, classical, mythological, and Biblical personages, which he claims to have read (24 stanzas); the "illnesses" of the kingdom under Juan II are described allegorically in the third section, consisting of fifteen stanzas; in the fourth division, Baena recalls the life and deeds of Alfonso VIII, and uses these facts as an example for Juan II (66 stanzas); the forty-six stanzas of the fifth part parallel Juan II's life with Alfonso's; Baena suggests "cures" for the kingdom's ills, and the remedies are personified, with the addition of a section in which the poet extols the virtues of Alvaro de Luna, whom he names as the herbolist who oversees the cures (42 stanzas); there follow eleven stanzas of the changes which will result from the properly administered remedies, and a conclusion of two stanzas plus the *finida*.

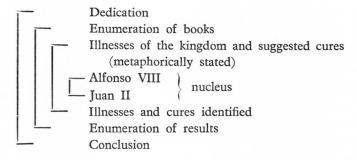

The two line dedication suggests the reason that Baena preferred not to include his long *dezir* in the *cancionero* he compiled: "Para Rey tan exçe-lente / perteneçe tal presente." It seems that since the work was presented as a gift to Juan II, and since it dealt so closely with the problems of the kingdom and the monarch's management of them, it would be improper for Baena to make public his opinions and advice. The intention of the poem is made quite clear from the beginning: the poet plans to alleviate the worries that are plaguing King Juan II at the time the poem was composed. But Baena fears that harsh criticism will result from what he is about to write:

---

12 Azáceta, *Cancionero de Baena*, I, p. xv.
13 Amador de los Ríos, *Historia*, VI, pp. 147-48, note 2.

... ...
avn que sepa çierta mente
que me quiebren bien la frente
por que fize este tractado,
... ...
nunca yo seré cobarde
por vos ser leal prouado.

Who are the "they" referred to in "quiebren?" Perhaps they were the king's advisors and other noblemen who were critics of the court, save Alvaro de Luna whom Baena later defends faithfully. Perhaps these men close to the king were suggesting other ways to rule the kingdom, or perhaps they were strongly opposed to Luna, the monarch's *privado*. Whatever the case, Baena is aware of their probable opposition to his opinions and he seeks the mercy and protection of Juan II. He also suggests that these noblemen heed what he writes, for they then would not find fault with his observations.

Before he begins to list the "illnesses" that Juan II's realm is suffering, Baena, who is also the court historian, offers a rather extensive list of the author's and works he claims to have read. He includes figures from ancient history to his contemporaries, and evens finds a place for mythology. The poet's enumeration recalls the classic poets and philosophers, the Bible and a number of its figures, scientific works, historical references to other countries, the Italians Dante and Boccaccio, and the history of Medieval Spain. Baena's allusions are indeed accurate, but it is doubtful that he actually read all the literature he mentions. What is more probable is a second-hand knowledge, that is, the poet read about these works and people in other forms and there-fore acquired his knowledge from secondary sources. His list of references approaches an impressive 100 in twenty-four stanzas. The primary purpose for offering such a list is, of course, to exhibit Baena's erudition. But the poet-historian might also have wanted his many references to past heroes to serve as a point of comparison with the contemporary figures he was about to mention: Juan II and Alvaro de Luna. His inspiration for this enumeration probably came from Dante, whose works he claims to be familiar with. The preoccupation with historical references, particularly allusions to ancient times, the idea of fame, his exaltation of Alvaro de Luna, and the comparison of Juan II to historical figures are ideas associated more with the Renaissance that with the Middle Ages. This Renaissance tendency, primitive as it may be in Baena's poem, is further developed about ten years later by Juan de Mena in his *Laberinto de Fortuna*. [14]

Once Baena has established credibility by revealing his familiarity with past occurrences, he begins the actual body of the *dezir* and embarks upon his stated purpose: to discuss the problems that are destroying Castile under the rule of Juan II. But Baena does not speak plainly of these conditions. Instead, the king's historian chooses to treat the circumstances as illnesses and writes of them in a totally metaphorical manner. Not once in this part of the poem does he refer to particular antagonists, battles, economic or political problems. The villains here are kidney disease, dropsy, toothache, and ague, accompanied by pains in the side, swelling of the lungs, and trembling. The cures, which Baena will later identify as people in the kingdom, are syrups, sugars, plasters, bleedings, and sweet-water baths. The most important aspects of the cure are a good doctor to prescribe the treatment, and a fine pharmacist to mix the necessary concoctions. The ten stanzas in which Baena describes the sickness that plagues the kingdom and suggests its treatment are indeed vague, for they reveal almost nothing about the real problems and do not offer real solutions. What, then, might have been Baena's intention? It seems that he is emphasizing the kingdom's weaknesses by comparing them to physical debilities, which are more readily understood by the reader. In addition, the poet calls attention to his literary capabilities, and holds the reader's interest in what promises to be a long treatise. Baena does not immediately reveal the meaning of his metaphors, but instead suggests the ultimate cure: follow the example of history. His transition from the "illnesses" to the deeds of Alfonso VIII of Castile is indeed graceful:

> Alto Rey: pues si queredes
> rreparar estas dolençias
> sin doctores nin çiençias
> y sin gastos que fazedes,
> Señor, cunple que notedes
> sotilmente mi rresponso,
> y lo qu'el Rey don Alfonso
> ouo fecho, vos faredes.

The sixty-six stanzas in which Baena discusses the life and deeds of Alfonso make up the largest single section of the poem, and together with the thirty-two that deal with the life of Juan II form the central part of the lengthy compo-

---

[14] The similarities that exist between Baena's *dezir* and Mena's *Laberinto* will be discussed below.

sition. In this historical passage, Baena carefully recounts with great accuracy that Alfonso inherited the throne as a child, and the dispute over his guardians and the kidnap that resulted from this struggle, his revenge against those who had wronged him, his defeat by the Moors, and the famous battle of Navas de Tolosa (1212). Alfonso finally resolves his problems with the kingdom of León by marrying his daughter to the monarch of that realm, and dividing the disputed territories between themselves. Baena then continues by recounting the early life of Juan II, comparing it, with great success, to Alfonso's childhood. Juan II, too, inherited the throne while still quite young, knew the dispute over who would have custody of him until he reached the age of majority, and was secuestered in Valladolid by his mother, Queen Catalina, who kept him there, for his own safety, for more than six years. Later, he was challenged by his cousins, the Infantes of Aragon, Enrique and Juan, and the struggle that followed lasted more than a decade. Thus, Baena uses the example of Alfonso VIII, who, under similar circumstances and apparent defeats, nevertheless finally knew success and fame for his deeds. History has served as the teacher.

It is important to note at this point that Baena's prologue to the *cancionero* he compiled deals in detail with the concept of history as example, and that it is very closely related to his use of historical reference in this *dezir*. In the beginning of the prose prologue, Baena establishes the importance of the past, stressing that it is the only point of time that man can truly know, because it has been completed. Baena further dwells on this concept, and expands the idea and its implications. Since the past is completely known, he explains, it can serve as an example for contemporary man, who can profit from its lessons on both good and evil. Even more important, the past can provide solutions to the present times' similar problems, and can be especially helpful to heads of state, who can employ to their own advantage the examples of former monarchs, who have already been proven successful or not:

> ... por que quando el semejante caso o casos les acaesçiere, que la su buena dispusiçion sea presta e aparejada para que puedan e sepan ser cabdillos e gouernadores, capitanes de grandes gentes, e que sepan con pura discreçion e con buen sseso gouernar e mandar e vedar e penar e asoluer e condenar e mantener e sostener en ordenança todas sus gentes e huestes e batallas e conquistas e guerras. ... E asymesmo pertenesçe mucho a los reyes e prinçipes e otros grandes señores de tener e leer e entender otros muchos libros e escrypturas de otras muchas manifycas e notables cosas, e de muy santas e prouechosas dotrynas, con las quales toman plaser e gassajado, e agradan mucho

las voluntades, e de mas rresçiben muchos ayusamientos buenos e prouechosos d'ellas. [15]

This passage can be directly applied to Baena's treatment of Alfonso VIII as an example for Juan II. The poet's obvious message to his king is to model his behavior after Alfonso's. Given the similar circumstances of the two monarch's early lives, the attacks which Alfonso's kingdom suffered and those that Juan's realm knew at the time, it seems only fitting that Castilla's contemporary king should be as successful as his predecessor if he would emulate his solutions. This advice, of course, proved to be incorrect: Juan II never knew such glory as did Alfonso VIII. To Baena, however, the suggestion seems quite logical. It is interesting to note that the poet employs this idea of history as teacher in approximately 1433, but does not verbalize the theory until 1445, when he apparently wrote the introduction to the *Cancionero de Baena*.

Once the nucleus of the poem is formed and the relationship between Alfonso and Juan is firmly established, Baena continues his composition by providing the details of the problems in the realm of his monarch. As mentioned above, this section of the *dezir* is parallel to the fifteen stanzas which preceded the life of Alfonso VIII, in which Baena described the conditions and the cures in metaphorical terms. In the next forty-two stanzas, the antagonists are identified, the solutions are proposed, and Alvaro de Luna is exalted. It seems that Castilla has been threatened by Juan II of Navarre and his brother Enrique, Maestre de Santiago, who were identified before as the Infantes de Aragón. Apparently, as was shown above, these two noblemen were suffering their final defeat in this matter at the time the poem was composed. Other antagonists include the ever-present Moors, whom Baena continuously refers to as pagan dogs, and the Infante Duarte of Portugal, who is accused of disloyalty to Juan II.

The cures mentioned above are now personified. Juan II's daughter, the Infanta, is capable of curing all with no more than her lovely face. The monarch's son, Enrique, who was to ascend the throne after his father's death in 1454, is chosen to administer the bleeding of the "patient." In addition, Baena suggests that Enrique be betrothed to the Infanta of Navarre, in order to solve the problems between the two kingdoms, just as Alfonso married his daughter to the king of Leon to achieve peace. Serving as soothing plasters are Juan II's counselors, Church prelates, and other wise men of the kingdom. The "patient" should also follow a diet of discrete persons, embassadors, loyal subjects, and should be bathed in the tears of the people. Since any medicine

---

[15] Azáceta, *Cancionero de Baena*, I, p. 11.

is more pleasantly administered with the addition of sugar, Baena adds to the prescription a dose of peace, to which he attributes such sweetness. The most important of all, as mentioned before, are the doctor and pharmacist, now identified as God and Alvaro de Luna. It is curious that Baena should dedicate but one stanza to the function of God as healer, and dwell on Luna for another eight. The poet takes this opportunity to extol the virtues of Luna, and to suggests that the *condestable* play a large role in helping the kingdom. While the exaltation of Alvaro de Luna is not the principal intention in Baena's *dezir,* or as important as it appears in Juan de Mena's *Laberinto de Fortuna,* it does seem to be of major concern in this composition.

Baena's work is now drawing to a close. He has enumerated the various problems that serve to destroy the kingdom, suggested that Juan II take heed of the successful example of Alfonso VIII, and has proposed other cures for the ailments. If his prescription is faithfully administered, the king can expect certain signs of regained health within his realm. Baena lists the probable results in the next eleven stanzas by enumeration using the future construction "çesarán" to denote an end to all the troubles. Among the effects to come, the poet mentions the end to the troublesome Portuguese, Navarrese, English, and Aragonese, along with relief for the poor and suffering people of the kingdom. Future greatness is suggested.

To conclude his long treatise, Baena again pleads with Juan II to affect the necessary changes "antes que entren los veranos" (which suggests that it was written in early 1433) "y sinon, lauo mis manos / y alço mano del juego." The poet has completed his proposed task, given the king the advice he deems necessary, and now realizes that he can do no more. He concludes with the familiar wish that God might bless and maintain the king, and that the king might consider the finished poem as a service to him.

From the descriptive treatment of Baena's long *dezir* it becomes apparent that this work bears an interesting, and perhaps important, resemblance to Juan de Mena's *Laberinto de Fortuna.* While Baena's poem is decidedly of a more primitive nature, it can indeed be compared to the *Laberinto* in its didactic intent, its political purpose, support of Alvaro de Luna, its episodic and historical structure, and treatment of past, present, and future. Although a period of more than ten years separates their dates of composition (about 1433 for Baena's *dezir,* 1444 for the Laberinto), the two works were obviously composed in the same atmosphere — the political confusion at the Castilian court of Juan II, and the rise to power of his *condestable,* Alvaro de Luna. Considering these various similarities, it would be worthwhile to compare more closely the two compositions.

The most obvious similarity between the poems by Baena and Mena is the narrative nature of the works, coupled with the length of the compositions. Until the *Laberinto* appeared in the mid-1440's, Baena's *dezir* was probably the longest poetic work of its kind in Spain. The historical, episodic framework of these two poems lends itself to lengthy dissertation. The manner in which the poets undertook their task differs, however. Mena treats past, present, and future at one time with his use of the three wheels: the wheel which represents the past is stationery, implying, as did Baena, that the past is finished and completely known; the wheels of the present and future are in constant motion, indicating the constant change that is occurring and the uncertainty of the outcome. Baena's plan, although it conveys the very same idea, is much more simplistic: his treatment is linear, his order is chronological. While Baena chooses only one example from history, a positive model, Mena employs many figures from the past as both positive and negative examples. In another instance, the two poets again treat the same premise in distinct manners. As we have seen, Baena enumerates historical and mythological figures in a series of stanzas at the beginning of his poem, without really explaining their meaning or importance. Mena, while he also uses a number of cultural references, integrates these allusions throughout the work, employing them in countless similes. For example, when Mena describes Alvaro de Luna in the order of Saturn, he refers to him as "que mucho en el cuerpo pareçe Tideo / y en el consejo Néstor el longeno." This technique of direct comparison of classical figures to contemporary personages implies, of course, a better command and understanding of what these characters represent. Certainly, it is more meaningful to relate one's knowledge of the past to things present, rather than to display this knowledge in a purely linear manner, as did Baena. In this way, the distinction between Mena's and Baena's treatment of the past and present phenomena can be easily discerned. Although the basic structure of time reference is present in Baena as it is in Mena, Baena can only integrate the past and present through the premise "Juan II = Alfonso VIII." In both poet's works, however, thematic integrity is not abandoned for lack or abundance of outside reference.

Once they have completed discussion of the past and present times, Baena and Mena turn to prophecy for the future. Since Providence has been the guide throughout Mena's allegory, it is she who predicts the outcome of the king's reign. The use of Providence as fortune teller also lends more credence and authority to the predictions that Mena chooses to present. The prophecy tells of Juan II's greatness which dims the fame of other kings, Spanish and foreign: "Será rey de reyes, señor de señores, / sobrando e vençiendo los títulos todos." In other words, Juan II can look forward to universal recognition and illustrious fame throughout history. Mena decides to elevate the position of Spain in the world by elevating its monarch to world glory. Baena, on the contrary, does not even consider such grand results. He is more concerned with the very immediate, more practical outcome of the king's application of astute methods to remedy the ills of his kingdom. What Baena foresees is an end to the problem of the Moors, a better relationship with the Portuguese, and an end to the suffering poor of the realm. Mena's King Juan II seems to owe his glory to his mere presence as monarch, while Baena's conception of a glorious king is one who earns his fame through loyalty to his subjects and diligence in political matters. Interestingly enough, Juan II was never capable of earning either poet's predicted glory. This difference in conception of the monarch and expected future greatness of the kingdom suggests the question of the poet's intent. What prompted Mena and Baena to write these two political-historical treatises?

Both Juan de Mena and Juan Alfonso de Baena had apparently been influenced to write the longs poems due to a sense of patriotism. The theme of national unity under Juan II is indeed present in both works. The optimistic conclusions predicting a glorious future or stability for Spain and the king is also included, along with the undeniably didactic intention. But while the two poets were moved by the same circumstances and intentions, they each had a different focus on the matter. That is to say, Baena's concern for the kingdom is more immediate, more urgent, more serious than the almost celestial aspirations presented by Mena. The basic difference between the two works is that Baena's *dezir* is firmly planted in medieval tradition, with its countless enumerations, its overt didacticism, its blatant moralizing, while Mena's *Laberinto* definitely tends toward a humanistic approach, with the inspiration in Dante. While the two works have in common the historical-episodic, narrative structure, political and national intention, praise of Alvaro de Luna, and some technical similarities such as the use of past-present-future and reference to historical and mythological figures, Mena's *Laberinto* is far more developed and rooted more in the Renaissance, although it maintains various medieval characteristics. Perhaps the more than ten-year separation of the dates of composition is in part responsible for the difference in the poet's application of knowledge, material, and intent. More probable is Mena's poetic talent, which outshines Baena's in depth and originality. It is interesting to note that because of both poet's relationship to the court (Baena's function as historian, Mena's as poet), Mena probably did know of Baena's *dezir* and may have used it as a primitive model for his own work, although Dante probably served him better.

As Juan Alfonso de Baena compiled his *cancionero,* he included in the epigraphs before each poem critical remarks about the composition. In addition to categorizing the works as *dezires, cantigas, preguntas,* etc., Baena often commented on how well or badly a poem was written, and what was particularly outstanding or poor about its artistry. In this way, he has given us a fine idea about what was considered proper form in this "arte de la gaya çiençia," for, indeed, the art was not without its rules of correct procedure. The majority of the compositions in the *Cancionero de Baena* are considered by its collector to be well written (since he obviously would not want to include inferior poetry in collection which would represent the poetic production of his time); only one poem stands out as being deemed "no bien fecho." [16] It was added to the *cancionero* because it was an answer to a *pregunta,* and was considered not well done because its meter varied from nine to twelve syllables per line, and the rhythm was quite clumsy. Other compositions are criticized when their rhyme scheme is broken, or their words do not rhyme properly. Baena's own *dezir,* not in this *cancionero* but in question, is not without fault, however. Baena may indeed have been a better literary critic than poet, if one may judge from the number of metric and rhyming inconsistencies found in the long poem.

On lines g and h of stanza 151, Baena makes the following observation about his composition: "sin falaça y sin diptongo / mis dichos metrificando." One becomes quite curious about what Baena understands as a diphthong. If he meant here that he does not rhyme diphthongs with single vowel sounds, he should be more modest about his poetic talents. Baena does in fact rhyme dipthongs with syllables containing but one vowel at least forty-seven times throughout the *dezir.* This can hardly be considered an accidental occurrence. This phenomenon appears most often in the "a" rhyme of the octaves (which have the scheme abbaacca). Of the four "a" rhymes, sometimes only one will be a diphthong (*despachado, injuriado, baruado, vengado,* of stanza 79); at times there are two diphthongs, two single vowels (*afruentas, tormentas, rrentas, cuentas* of stanza 63); occasionally there will be but one single vowel sound surrounded by three blends (*çimiento, fundamiento, testamento, tiento,* of stanza 15). Sometimes Baena even rhymes two different diphthongs that have the same strong vowel (*Atiença* and *verguença* of stanza 75); different diphthongs that rhyme also appear in the company of single vowel sounds

---

[16] Poem 123, *Cancionero de Baena.*

(*ledo, denuedo, miedo, Toledo* of stanza 120). So Baena can hardly boast the lack of this kind of rhyme in his *dezir*.

Consonantal rhyme is also of interest in this poem. On four occasions, Baena allows two consonants to "blend" to rhyme with a single consonant. In stanza 4, *digno* and *chino* rhyme; stanza 5 contains *someto, recto, perfecto, secreto*; also rhyming are *Piramos* and *anbos, magna* and *soberana*. The question is, of course, whether these words did actually rhyme when spoken. Though they probably did not coincide perfectly in their sounds, the proximity of their pronunciation apparently made their "rhyme" acceptable.

There are five cases in this *dezir* in which the words in question do not rhyme at all. In stanza 87, *aguinaldo* does not rhyme with *andando, errando, vando*, although the variant *aguilando* does appear in other poems of the era, and may have been meant but mistaken by the copyist. Stanza 113 contains *seña, Gascueña, Armeña*, and unfortunately also *Borgoña*, an error that most likely cannot be blamed on the copyist. On two occasions, the poet uses what seems to be assonant rhyme, which does not coincide with his overall scheme of consonance: *contemplad, andar, pensar*, and *pesar* of stanza 159; *agua* and *flama* of stanza 166. *Contrarios* of stanza 163 does not even approach the rhyme set by *enemigos, amigos, testigos*.

Two stanzas of the *dezir* are so problematic as to their rhyme scheme as to make them almost impossible to correct. The last two lines of stanza 47 are missing, and the rhyme as it stands is abcaad—, showing little promise for reconstruction. A very strange case is that of stanzas 131 and 132. The scheme of 131 is abcaadda; that of 132 is abbccddc. Their "a" and "c" rhymes are the same, suggesting a possible relationship between the two strophes, probably a confusion of their lines. However, each stanza in itself makes grammatical sense, and it is not evident which lines may have been switched, if any at all.

The meter of Baena's *dezir* also has its inconsistencies. While the poem is meant to be octosyllabic, lines of seven and nine syllables abound. Twenty-four verses have nine syllables, although some may be attributed to error of the copyist. Five of these lines (18c, 19f, 64e, 211h, 219c) begin with the word "y" which may easily be deleted without a change of meaning to the verse. It seems that the "y" may have been added gratuitously by the copyist, not an error attributable to the poet. This still leaves, however, nineteen times in which Baena could have polished his poetry a bit more. There are fifty lines that have only seven syllables, but the addition of a written dierisis can change forty-one of these to octosyllabic lines. One verse, 167h, needed the addition of two dierises. Line 157h is quite deficient, with but six syllables.

The orthography is as variable as one could expect for the fifteenth century, but there is a great amount of consistency. An interesting note in the constant spelling of *rreyes* (as one would expect it to appear) without the last "e" (*rreys*). The word is pronounced, however, with two syllables, as judged from the meter of the poem. In one instance, the copyist writes *leys* to rhyme with *rreys,* and it, too, has two syllables.

The following edition of Jnan Alfonso de Baena's untitled *dezir* is based on the complete text of the poem found in the *Cancionero de San Román.* Because of the fragmentary nature of the version of the composition in the *Cancionero de Palacio,* MS. 593, it is not a reliable source. The critical edition presented here is true to the original text, with the following modifications: abbreviations have been resolved; capitalization and punctuation have been added to facilitate reading; obvious copyist's errors have been corrected, but noted in the "Notes to the Edition" that follows the text; "R," where it occurs in a normally uncapitalized word, has been resolved as "rr."

The poem has also been annotated: of the many references made by Baena in this long *dezir,* the obvious have been left without annotation (e.g., Plato, Virgil, Hercules); the more uncommon references have been explained. This section also points out any irregularities in the text, such as omission of lines or change in the order of the verses.

The translation of this poem is presented in prose because of the apparent difficulty of reconstructing poetry in another language. The English is as close in meaning as possible to the original Spanish. There were, however, problems translating certain medieval Spanish words which have since fallen into disuse.

DEZIR QUE FIZO
JUAN ALFONSO DE BAENA

1   Para Rey tan exçelente
    perteneçe tal presente.

2   Alto Rey muy soberano
    de los rreynos de Castilla,
    asentado en rrica silla
    como noble palaçiano:
    rrescibit en vuestra mano
    este escrito muy plaziente
    que vos da con buen talente
    vuestro seruidor fulano.

3   Alto Rey: si bien leedes
    y notaes mi proçeso,
    solamente vn exçeso
    del açento non veredes;
    antes creo que tomedes
    grant plazer y gasajado,
    pues con el será aliuiado
    el trabajo que oy tenedes.

4   Alto Rey: los protestantes,
    segun que dispone el digno
    Juan Andres Bartolo, Chino,
    son de carga rreleuantes;
    y por ende en consonantes
    al comienço aquí protesto,

2*d*. Although the word "palençiano" appears in the manuscript, "palaçiano" seems more appropriate.

4*c*. Bartolo: famous Italian jurisconsult of the fourteenth century, whose legal works dominated in the universities of that time.

que yo fundo todo aquesto
sobre los rreys y infantes.

5   Alto Rey: yo me someto
so vuestra merçet y amparo
por quanto lo que declaro
es vuestro seruiçio rrecto;
y quien calla bien perfecto
a su rrey en tal estrecho
non paresçe ser bien fecho;
aqui yaze gran secreto.

6   Alto Rey: maguer en Deça
tienen vso mucho malo
que le den con gordo palo
al que trota si estrapieça;
y tanbien aca en Baeça
vsan de otras nesçedades
al que dize las verdades
que le quiebren la cabeça.

7   Alto Rey, Señor loado:
avn que sepa çierta mente
que me quiebren bien la fruente
por que fize este tractado,
o que sepa ser quemado
como leña que bien arde,
nunca seré yo cobarde
por vos ser leal prouado.

8   Alto Rey: ca es fundado
por seruir los muy derecho
y por onrra y por prouecho
de todo vuestro rreynado;
por los qual, Rey esmerado,
si lo bien rreconosçedes
ya soy çierto que merçedes
me avredes muy de grado.

9   Alto Rey: rruego y pido
a los nobles en condiçiones,
fidalgos lindos varones
de linaje muy escogido,
que non pongan en oluido

de notar mi escritura,
a vn buen fin e sin mestura
como en ella es contenido.

10   Alto Rey: maguer conquisto
yo seré de arguyentes,
envidiosos maldezientes
mi tratado bien rreuisto;
pero juro en Jesucristo
esto que de por fazaña,
que jamas en toda España
otro tal nunca fue visto.

11   5v   Pues escuchen los señores
y Infantes y perlados,
duques, condes, adelantados,
los maestros y priores,
mariscales, rregidores
de çibdades y de villas:
oyan todos marauillas,
non se espanten trobadores.

12   Escuchen pues castellanos,
grandes savios rremonistas
y sotiles alquimistas,
y los rrudos aldeanos,
judios, moros, cristianos,
frayres, monges, omes legos,
coxos, mancos, mudos, çiegos:
tajen plumas escriuanos.

13   Y rremiren los artistas
d'aquesta çiençia gaya,
cada punto con su rraya
sin ojos llenos de aristas;
y los muy grandes sofistas
noten bien sy ay falaçia,
ca sin falta sin sagaçia
fundaré mis obras mistas.

14   Yo leý plana por plana,
avn que soy mal coronista,

11b.   "Pelados" appears in the manuscript, but seems to be an error of the copyist.

la famosa y grant conquista
de la grant çibdat troyana:
y otrosi la rromana
coronica de gentiles,
y las estorias sotiles,
tripartita e tusculana.

15   Yo leý bien de çimiento
la grant General Estoria,
rretoue en la memoria
como va su fundamiento;
sobtel Viejo Testamento
de la ley vieja y nueua,
la qual es tan fonda cueua
que no sé quien tome tiento.

16   Yo leý en el Vegeçio
que conpuso las batallas,
el que sopo asi pintallas
y las puso en gran presçio;
Tito Livios y Boeçio,
en el Seneca y Lucano;
estos libros que desplano
non los leý como nesçio.

17   Yo leý en el Caton
y al poeta sabio Dante,
en Ovidio el Ylustrante,
en Virgilio, en Platón;
en el muy sotil Remon,
en el Omero y en el Novato,
en Rogel y en Policrato,
en Ricardo y en Celon.

18   Yo leý en los morales
de Aristotiles el Sabio,
y las batallas de estrolabio,
y de Oclides y Natales;

17f. Novato: Carthaginian schismatic priest of the third century, of exceedingly bad reputation, above all for his avarice.

17h. Ricardo: Spanish writer and prelate of the seventh century, author of the *Regla* for the nuns of the Order of Saint John of Malta.

18c. Batallas de estrolabio: perhaps this refers in some way to Strabo, the Greek geographer.

y leý los purismales
que rrelata Juan Bocaçio;
de Mocrovio y de Oraçio
sus libros filosofales.

19   Yo leý grandes poetas
y a Tulio y a Tiberio,
a Zarquel y al grant Valerio,
y otras leturas netas
sobre el sol y las planetas
y de sus rrayos corrusantes,
muy claros y rrutilantes
de estrellas y de cometas.

20   Yo leý de Limosines
sus candençias logicales,
de las artes liberales,
prosas, cantos y latines;
y leý los saradines
que conpuso Roma y guia,
y los montes de Torquia
en cançiones florentines.

21   6r   Yo leý la pelegrina
partidas y ordenamientos,
y fueros y rregimientos
y la suma de Anbrosina;
y mas la ley Bartolina
y los libros rretretantes
de çiençias espantantes,
de la peña cumasina.

22   Yo leý dentro en Baena,
do aprendí fazer borrones
y comer alcaparrones
muchas vezes sobre çena;

19b. Tiberio (Tiberius): second Roman Emperor, 42 B.C. to 37 A.D., author of lyric poetry.

19c. Valerio (Valerius maximus): Latin historian of the first century, author of nine books of famous sayings and deeds.

20a. Limosines: the inhabitants of Limoges, an old province of France.

21b, c. Baena is apparently referring to the *Siete Partidas* and *Fuero Juzgo* of Alfonso X, el Sabio.

21e. "Ley bartolina": evidently a reference to Bartolo (see note to 4c).

y los libros de Abiçena
y sus rrectos inforismos;
Alto Rey: mis silogismos
fazen fin, mas al rretruena.

23   Alto Rey: muchos torneos
yo leý en las estorias
que ovieron en vitorias
Müysen son sus ebreos;
son Judas los macabeos
y del justo y grand varon
Josue, y avn de Sanson
que mató los filisteos.

24   Yo leý que Gedeon
fizo lides mucho fuertes
que dïeron crudas muertes
a los del Rey Faraon;
de Saul y Salamon
y del Santo Rey Dauid,
que vido matar en lid
a su buen fijo Absalon.

25   Yo leý del señorio
del muy grant Rey Alixandre,
segunt cuenta Sant Leandre
que vençio el poderio
del Rey Dario con su brio,
y conquistó todo el mundo,
tierra y mar y su prefundo,
el diziendo: "Todo es mio."

26   Yo leý con grand deseo
las batallas muy campales
que ovieron tan mortales
Jullio Cesar y Ponpeo;
y de aquel Rey Tolomeo
y Anibal el Africano,
de Cipion, de Trajano,
grandes cosas d'ellos leo.

_____

25c. Sant Leandre: Archbishop of Seville c.66, brother of Saint Isidore.
26e. Tolomeo: Ptolemy XIV.

27   Yo leý la espantable
y cruel guerra de Troya,
do se perdio tanta joya
y gentio inumerable;
y morió el venerable
poderoso Rey Piramos,
y los dos sus fijos anbos,
Paris, Ector el Notable.

28   Yo leý, pero con pena,
el rrey noble desque muerto
que mataron a grant tuerto
a su fija, Poliçena.
¡O maldita seas, Elena,
con toda su fermosura
que senbraste tal tristura,
non feziste como buena!

29   Yo leý que fue solada
la çibdat toda por suelo,
y se fizo muy grand duelo
desque vieron ser rrobada
la muy linda enamorada
del buen cauallero Archiles,
que por manos crueles viles
de Pirro fue degollada.

30   Yo leý en la perdiçion
d'esta Troya cosas feas,
fechas todas por Eneas
dentro del gran Elïon;
ca vendió el Paladion
a los griegos Menalao,

27f. Priamos (Priam): last king of Troy, father of Paris and Hector (27h).

28d. Poliçena (Polyxena): daughter of Priam, whose intention to marry Achilles was opposed by her brother Hector. She was sacrificed at the tomb of Achilles.

29f. Arquiles (Achilles): he killed Hector and was slain by Paris.

29h. Pirro (Pyrrhus or Neoptoʾemus): son of Achilles, who slew Priam and wielded the knife when Polyxena was sacrificed.

30d. Elion (Illion); Greek name for Troy.

30e. Paladion (Palladium): statue of Athena. The safety of the city supposedly depended on the preservation of this statue.

30f. Menalao (Menalaus): husband of Helen of Troy, who took her back to Sparta after the war.

desque vio Elena en su nao
alçó velas de rrendon.

31   6v   Yo leý del capitan
y grant duque de Bullon,
de Narçiso y de Jason,
d'Ercoles y de Roldan,
Carlos Manos y Florestan,
de Amadis y Lançarote,
Valdouin y Camelote,
de Galas y de Tristan.

32   Yo leý del Taburlan
muy mayor que Costantino
nin que Marco nin Latino
y mayor que Preste Juan;
y leý del grand soldan
y del muy fuerte Morato,
y de otros que non rrelato
que fueron despues de Adan.

33   Yo leý de aquestos todos,
del conde Fernant Gonçales,
del buen Cid y de otros tales
que follaron muchos lodos
por guardarlo que los godos
ganaron en tienpos antigos;
y leý del Rey Rodrigo
terribles cosas y modos.

34   Yo leý que guerreando
los rreys de las Españas
fezieron grandes fazañas
muchas tierras conquistando,
de los quales vó rrezando

31b. Duque de Buillon (Godfried, Duke of Bouillon): duke of Lower Lorraine (1061-1100), director of the first Crusade, and the first king of Jerusalem.
31e, f, g, h. Characters of novels of chivalry.
32a. Taburlan: perhaps Tamerlaine, the Tartan conqueror.
32c. Marco: possibly Marcus Aurelius.
32c. Latino: king of the Aborigenes in the *Aeneid.* Eneas fought Turuno to win the hand of Latino's daughter, Livinia.
33g. Rodrigo (Roderic): last Visigothic king in Spain, conquered by the Moors in 711.

algunos d'ellos en suma,
como quiera que mi pluma
de escreuir se va enojando.

35   Yo leý, quiero dezilla,
su nobleza de dos rreys
que fezieron nobles leys
y fechos de marauilla:
don Ferrnando y su quadrilla
que ganó con sus bondades
a las muy nobles çibdades
de Cordoua y de Seuilla.

36   Yo leý, maguer somero,
de Algeziras y su alcayde,
la de Alcala de Bençayde
que ganó el buen guerreo
don Alfonso el Postrimero,
que asi ouo este nonbre,
el qual fue mas gentil onbre
que nasçio despues de Nero.

37   Yo leý, abreuiando,
de algunos predesçedores
que fueron enperadores,
pero dexo de yr nonbrando;
desde el mano don Fernando
fasta el grant conquistador,
nieto del enperador,
don Alfonso, otros dexando.

38   Alto Rey: aqui parando
mi obra metreficante,
non quise mas adelante
yr de otros rrelatando;
mas en esto me fundando
en los fechos que fezieron,

35e. Ferrnando: Fernando III, the Saint (1199-1252).
36c. Alcala de Bençayde (Aben-Zaide): when this Moorish city was reconquered in 1341, Alfonso XI renamed it "Alcalá la Real," which it has retained.
36h. It is very curious that Baena should refer to Nero as "gentil."
37e. Fernando I, the Great, King of Castilla, Leon and Navarra (1035-1065).
37h. Alfonso VIII of Castilla (1155-1214).

los rreys que d'el venieron
feo es pasar callando.

39   Alto Rey: ya só cansado
y tanbien cansa mi lengua,
como quier que fize mengua
y meresco ser culpado
por que non conté acabado
de los otros tan famosos
rreys, santos glorïosos,
pero sea me perdonado.

40   Alto Rey: ca non fiz esto
por menguar papel nin tinta,
nin tanpoco por infinta
que los non leý tan presto;
pero fue por que sobresto
non conplió que mas nonbrase,
saluo ende que tornase
a lo al que faz al testo.

41   7r   Alto Rey: pues que mis çejas
socarré tanto leyendo,
es rrazon que concluyendo
yo dé fin a mis consejas;
pues escuchen las orejas
de todos los que vos aman,
y verán que no me llaman
Pasqual Gil de las ouejas.

42   Alto Rey: segund la trama
vuestro rreyno está doliente
de tan grand açidente
que mas arde que la llama;
o maguera que rreclama
nunca falla quien se duela,
y con dolor de la muela
dias ha que fuerte brama.

43   Alto Rey: non fue purgado
por la forma que deuía
nin curado por la via

41h. Pascual Gil: apparently a name used by Baena to refer to a peasant.

que deuiera ser rreglado;
por lo qual quedó achacado
y muy lleno de vmores,
que le dan asas tremores
y dolor en el costado.

44   Alto Rey: ya era sana
la çeçion de Palençuela,
mas dolando aquesta çuela
rrevolvio la conterçiana;
Dios lo guarde de quartana
por que non venga rrotura,
y muy rrezia callentura
le venga cotidïana.

45   Alto Rey: sin las syçiones
ay otras señas cïertas
de dolençia encubiertas
que ya tiene en los riñones;
ca le finchan los pulmones
y rresçela perlezia,
sy rrecresçe ytropesia
es señal de perdiçiones.

46   Alto Rey: los sus ardores
y dolençias tan esquiuas
cada dia son mas biuas
y mas frescas y peores;
y ya sueñas sus dolores
y rrevuelvan como viento,
y d'ello an sentimiento
papas, rreys, enperadores.

47   Alto Rey: si luego enpunto
non le acorren los maestros
muy profundos y bien discretos
el vmor será mas junto;
ca, Señor, segunt barrunto
este mal de luengo viene
... ...
... ...

_47g, h._ In the manuscript, the copyist left space for two lines, but never wrote them in.

48   Alto Rey: para los daños
d'estas guerras y peleas,
grandes males, grandes preas,
començadas con sosaños,
para tunbos tan estraños
y de tan crudos negoçios
eran menester sicroçios
muy leales sin engaños.

49   Alto Rey: y melezinas
de almivar con arropes,
de rruyvarbo los xaropes
y triacas mucho finas;
açucar de girofrinas,
y comer buenas viandas
y poner vnturas blandas
por do salgan las espinas.

50   Alto Rey: de otras vias
enplastos para los lomos
que rrefrien mas que plomos
y otras semientes frias;
otrosi buenas sangrias,
sobre todo algunos vaños
de agua dulçe de los caños
por que salgan azedias.

51   7v   Alto Rey: fin de rrazones
era menester vn grande
fisico para que mande
ordenar las purgaçiones;
otrosi fuego y caruones
y vn sabio buticario,
muy profundo erbolario
que faga las decoçiones.

52   Alto Rey: pues si queredes
rreparar estas dolençias
sin doctores nin çiençias
y sin gastos que fazedes,
Señor, cumple que notedes

50c, d. These verses appear in the order d, c, in the manuscript, and are reversed
here to preserve the original rhyme.

sotilmente mi rresponso,
y lo qu'el rrey don Alfonso
ouo fecho, vos faredes.

53   Alto Rey: non es fallado
por escrito nin por ley,
que en el mundo fuese rrey
tanto tienpo afortunado,
nin de tantos conquistado;
enpero maguer corrido,
de Dios fue bien socorrido
y non fue desanparado.

54   Alto Rey: este nonbrado
segunt dizen fue su nieto
del enperador discreto,
don Alfonso muy famado;
y fue fijo del onrrado
Rey don Sancho que adorauan,
y todas las gentes llamauan
el Rey Santo Deseado.

55   Alto Rey: niño chequito
este rrey quedó moçuelo
de quatro años pequeñuelo
y muy graçioso y bendito;
el diablo vil maldito
començó de armar su lidia
de maldad y mucha enbidia
por la forma que rrepito.

56   Alto Rey: fue consejado
a su tio, Rey de Leon,
don Fernando, grant follon,
que su rreyno ajuntado
fuese todo derramado
por Castilla, y que rrobasen
a todo quanto fallasen
en el canpo y en el poblado.

57   Alto Rey: falsos rruynes
que lo tal le consejaron

54f. Sancho III of Castilla (1157-1158).
56b, c. Fernando II, King of Leon (1157-1188).

de tal guisa lo enrridaron
qu'el creyó a los malsines;
lo que fizo a dos fines
por qu'el rreyno se gastase,
y despues que lo cobrase,
sin gritar, muchos florines.

58   Alto Rey: sin detenençia
asy fue por obra puesto,
ca su tio el rrey dispuesto
sin temor y sin conçiençia
trabajó don grant famençia
por razer muchos portillos
en las villas y castillos
del rrey niño con treuençia.

59   Alto Rey: estos males
que Castilla d'el sufria,
leuantóse grant porfia
entre los santos seruiçiales
por saber a que ofiçiales
se daría la tomança
del rrey niño y su criança
lucharon sobre puñales.

60   Alto Rey: y fue dexado
a don Gutierre de Castro
y minaronle por rrastro
por lo qual le fue quitado;
y fue luego entregado
al grand conde don Enrrique,
de quien ay tan gran pedrique
a que soy muy espantado.

61   8r   Alto Rey: despues fue dado
aquel niño por grant plaça
a don Garçia de Daça,
ome muy desuenturado;
por lo qual fue rrequestado
entre Castro y los de Lara

60b. Gutierre de Castro; 60f. Enrrique; 61c. Garcia de Daça; 66c. Manrrique;
74f. Nuño: these men were apparently figures of the court of Alfonso VIII.

y quebrada mucha vara
por quien tomaria el estado.

62 Alto Rey: mucho temiendo
don Enrrique aquestas cosas
que serien muy peligrosas,
don Fernando al rrey beniendo;
ca velando y dormiendo
al rrey niño rrobaria,
o que gelo tomaria,
fuese a Soria con el fuyendo.

63 Alto Rey: tales tormentas
ouo el rreyno aquella vez
que fue negra mas que pez
la suma de sus afruentas;
ca tomó todas las rrentas
el rrey niño doze años,
y lançó grandes rrabaños
de otros pechos sin dar cuentas.

64 Alto Rey: en su letura
d'este niño perseguido,
se rrecuenta muy conplido
que ovo fuerte ventura;
y don Enrrique tan quexura
que maguera grant fidalgo,
otorgó si diesen algo
que daria el niño con jura.

65 Alto Rey: en mal oraje
don Enrrique asi acusado,
y del rrey niño apremiado
leuantóse en mal puntaje;
y fizo pleyto y omenaje
que la mano le besase
a su tio y otorgase
el rrey niño vasallaje.

66 Alto Rey: luego partió
para Soria el rrey cruel,
y don Manrrique con el
por que asi lo prometió;
y al punto que y llegó

demandó qu'el niño diese,
por que luego se conpliese
la postura qu'el juró.

67   Alto Rey: los que guardauan
al rrey niño con desmayo
en los braços de su ayo
delante el todos llorauan;
y planiendo, sospirando
por aquella aleuosia
y tan mala pletesia
que del rrey niño trataua.

68   Alto Rey: todos dexieron:
"O Santa Maria val,
tal error y tanto mal
los nasçidos non lo vieron;
a nos libre nos le dieron
del rrey asi lo damos,
a vos, Conde, lo entregamos."
Y del rrey se despidieron.

69   Alto Rey: con ardideza
vn fidalgo buen vasallo
caualgó en vn cauallo
y fizo grant sotileza;
furtó el niño sin pereza
y leuólo so vna capa,
bien corriendo a la trapa
a Gormaz la fortaleza.

70   Alto Rey: en que no daua
el rrey niño y non salia,
su mal tio alli fazia
grant rruydo y rrenegaua;
y con seña se tornaua
al buen conde con bravura,
por el pleyto y postura
pues el niño non le daua.

71   8v   Alto Rey: fue detenido
el rrey crudo en dilaçiones,
ca poniendole defensiones
que era el niño adormeçido;

pero fue le rrespondido
dende a poco con manera,
que vn ome que y veniera
con el niño avrá foydo.

72   Alto Rey: fue ya sentido
por el tio muy yrado,
como el niño era furtado
y fincó muy desmayado
por que fue mal escarnido
del buen conde y su promesa;
por lo qual acaesçió desa
alli en Soria grant rroydo.

73   Alto Rey: muy despegado
partió dende el rrey tirano
por que el niño rrey loçano
escapó y fue librado;
fuese el muy enojado,
protestando todavia
que por todos noche y dia
el niño fuese buscado.

74   Alto Rey: los dos hermanos
del buen conde trabajaron
de manera que fincaron
del error linpios y sanos;
ca trotó cuestas y llanos
el leal conde don Nuño,
fasta que sacó en el puño
al niño de entre villanos.

75   Alto Rey: sin grant fardaje
dio con el dentro en Atiença;
sin temor y sin vergüença
envió bien que su linaje
del mal pleyto y desagaje
con aquesto lo saluaua;
pues qu'el rrey niño libraua
de poder del rrey saluaje.

76   Alto Rey: luego fue puesta
a don Manrrique demanda
por el rrey quando non blanda

mas rrebato que non rrequesta,
que veniese a dar rrespuesta
de la su mala verdad,
y perjuró de falsedad
que la lid que estaua presta.

77   Alto Rey: fue orgulloso
don Manrrique en rrespondiendo,
y su onrra defendiendo
dixo al rrey mucho sañoso:
"Yo non fui nin só aleuoso,
nin traydor nin fee mentido,
mas meresco ser tenido
por leal y grandioso."

78   Alto Rey: fue delibrado
aquel pleyto por jüyzio
que non fizo prejüyzio
don Manrrique, nin fue errado;
ante fue determinado
que libró de seruidunbre
a su rrey y le dio lunbre
y devia ser coronado.

79   Alto Rey: ya despachado
don Manrrique d'esta presa
leuantóse otra enpresa
del rrey niño injuriado;
dende a poco fue baruado
y punó por auer onrra,
y de quien ouo desonrra
por su punto fue vengado.

80   Alto Rey: el niño bueno
don Alfonso muy gentil,
esmerado entre çient mill,
este noble rrey noueno,
luego andouo por su rreyno
non caçando con falcones
mas buscando los ladrones
espantando mas que trueno.

81   9r   Alto Rey: el grant cuydado
que tenia y malencolia

> por el rrobo y tirania
> que su tio avia vsado;
> esto lo fizo forçado
> apretar las enpulgueras
> como toro en barreras
> es corrido y garrochado.

82
> Alto Rey: ca muy de cote
> y con seña muy ardientes
> a los rreys sus parientes
> mal los traxo al estricote;
> quien comió el almodrote
> y su rreyno le gastaron
> al fin desque yantaron
> bien pagaron el escote.

83
> Alto Rey: luego primero
> començó a fazer estrena
> y vengóse a boca llena
> de su tio el tortiçero;
> como rrey muy justiçiero
> le corrió bien la çapata
> por el rrobo y la barata
> que le fizo el viejo trotero.

84
> Alto Rey: despues vençiólo
> en el canpo muchas vezes,
> y llególo a las fezes
> de fincar sin gente solo;
> finalmente conquistólo
> y tomóle sus lugares
> que el tenia y sin vagares
> fasta ser muerto corriólo.

85
> Alto Rey: desque finado
> su mal tio manzillero
> a su fijo el heredero
> non lo dexó oluidado;
> apretó con el priado
> y corrióle la cuxia

82e, f. In the manuscript, these two verses appear in the order f, e, and are inverted here to coincide with the established rhyme scheme.

85c. His "fijo heredero" was Enrique I.

y rrasgól' su almexia
y dexólo desonrrado.

86   Alto Rey: ya rrequestados
padre y fijos y venidos,
desonrrados y perdidos
y de sus rregnos echados,
corriólos tierras y prados
de Nauarra al Rey Sancho,
que tenie su rreyno ancho
de lugares mal ganados.

87   Alto Rey: asy andando
este niño fuerte y brauo
non presçió solo vn clauo
a los qu'el fueron errando;
nin dexó son aguinaldo
Aragon que a toda boça
le rrasgó bien la coroça
a su rrey con su gran vando.

88   Alto Rey: muy infingido
Portogal tañie su tronpa,
y magier tiene grant ponpa
por estar muy bastesçido,
este rrey muy atreuido
le corrió bien la canpiña
y dexólos con grant tiña
mucho triste y dolorido.

89   Alto Rey: asi follados
sus contrario d'esta guisa,
començó a fazer pesquisa
contra los muy rrenegados
moros falsos encartados,
y ganóles luego a Cuenca
y los prados de Yberlenca,
que son oy pueblos çerrados.

90   Alto Rey: desque se vido
este niño asi encarnando,
en los moros ya çenando
y se vio brauo y temido,
dio estonçes grant bramido

por ganar onrra y prez,
y juró que fasta Fez
llegaría su apellido.

91   9v   Alto Rey: como tenia
este rrey grant coraçon
y demas buena entençion
por que a Dios seruir queria,
el afin que asolaria
a los moros, perros canes,
començando tomar afanes
y seguillos con porfia.

92   Alto Rey: fue para Alarcos
y fue mucho en ora mala,
con su gente puesta en ala
de cauallo y a pie con arcos;
ca salieron de los charcos
çient mill moros en alcançe,
y matando a todo trançe
fue de alli sin rred y barcos.

93   Alto Rey: desque arrancado
fue corrido çinco leguas
de los moros sin dar treguas,
y muy bien acuchillado;
enpero non fue tomado
de los moros sin guerreros,
ca sobióse en los oteros
onde fue bien anparado.

94   Alto Rey: el bien quesiera
a los moros darles vuelta
y tornar a rrienda suelta
farre dentro y farre fuera;
mas enbidia con dentera
de los rreys sus vezinos
enbidiosos y malinos,
le enbargaron la carrera.

95   Alto Rey: mas que la yel
este rrey y quebrantado

92a. Alarcos: hill in the province of Ciudad Real. Alfonso VIII was defeated there by the Moor Almanzor in 1195, the event referred to in this stanza.

y por ser desbaratado
leuantáronse contra el;
de enemigos grant tropel
por fallar tienpo que achaque,
füeron dar con vn vaque
todo a fin de aforrar d'el.

96   Leuantóse luego pendon
Portogal amenazando;
leuantóse rrenegando
su primo, rrey de Leon;
leuantóse de mal son
el Rey Sancho nauarrisco;
leuantóse con pedrisco
Rey Alfonso de Aragon.

97   Leuantóse de Granada
el rrey moro y los gomeres;
leuantóse de Alhameres
mucha gente rrenegada;
leuantóse en asonada
otro rrey con serrazines;
leuantóse de marines
toda la tierra quajada.

98   Leuantóse de paganos
otro rrey de los alarabes;
leuantóse començarabes,
el rrey turco y espianos;
leuantóse de africanos
vn cabdillo de Almohardes;
leuantáronse alcaydes
mas espesos que milanos.

99   Leuantáronse eso mysmo
en su rreyno esas tizones;
leuantáronse cabrones
y carçeles del abismo;

96d. Rey de Leon: the aforementioned Alfonso IX.
96f. Rey Sancho: Sancho VII, the Strong, of Navarra (1194-1234).
96h. Alfonso II of Aragon (1162-1196).
98f. Almohardes (Almohades): Arabic dynasty that reigned in Andalusia from
1147-1269.

leuantáronse en cristianismo
contra el tantos contrallos
que non podrian contallos
por la cuenta de alguarismo.

100   Alto Rey: asi çercado
de enemigos capitales
este rrey, tantos y tales
como suso he rrecontado,
con tristeza y grant cuydado
non podia tomar plazer;
non sabia que se fazer
mas cuydó ser asolado.

101   *101r*   Alto Rey: curó de auer
su consejo y buen acuerdo
este rrey, como ome cuerdo
con la rreyna su mugier;
otrosi quiso saber
de los suyos que lo amauan,
el consejo que le dauan
para aquel grant menester.

102   Alto Rey: ningun arrimo
non falló nin otro anparo
este rrey, para en rreparo
de sus cuytas y lastimo,
saluo este que esprimo:
que fue dar su linda fija
por muger con la sortija
al rrey de Leon, su primo.

103   Alto Rey: los dos amores
luego en punto lo juntaron,
y por cortes los casaron
con mill justas y atanbores;
el rrey noble de valores
egualó las cosas todas,
y fechas las rricas bodas
byuieron a sus sabores.

101d. Alfonso VIII's wife, Eleanor of England.
102g. "Su linda fija": Alfonso's daughter, Berenguela, married Alfonso IX of Leon.

104 Alto Rey: esto acabado,
quedaron bien egualados:
suegro y yerno muy pagados
y todo el rrigor quitado;
el rrey noble y rredotado
los lugares que ganara
a su yerno y le tomara
el gelos tornó de grado.

105 Alto Rey: fueron pesantes
los rreys sus comarcanos,
por que vieron tan çercanos
suegro y yerno en los talantes;
ca se vieron mal andantes
por qu'el rrey les tornaria
a correr y estruyria
como les feziera d'antes.

106 Alto Rey: por que fincasen
los negoçios mas seguros
con firmeza de altos muros
para sienpre y non quebrasen;
y juraron que guardasen
aquestos dos solos puntos,
que Castilla y Leon juntos
en vn rreyno se tornasen.

107 Alto Rey: en arte estraña
fizo mas como maestro
este rrey, lo que demuestro:
amansó su yra y saña,
lo que syenpre turba y daña;
fizo pleytos y posturas
y sus pazes y sus juras
a los moros con grant maña.

108 Alto Rey: asi firmados
estos tractos con firmezas,
començó a fazer proezas
este rrey en sus rregnados;
fizo en Burgos muy dotados

106g, h. The year was 1230.

las huelgas con ospital,
lo qual non faze otro tal
ningunt rrey de los pasados.

109   Alto Rey: diz la materia
del prouerbio acostunbrado,
que se dize muy notado:
"En cada lugar y feria
el que pasa grant lazeria,
o el que con manzilla biue,
nunca duerme, mas escriue
en su coraçon miseria."

110   Alto Rey: por semejante
non se le oluidó vn rrato
la desonrra y el desvarato
que este rrey oviera ante;
y por verse mal andante
y de los moros vençido,
sienpre estouo aperçibido
por vengarse bien auante.

111 *10v*   Alto Rey: obra famada
este rrey fizo en tanto:
suplicó al Padre Santo
por auer d'el cruzada,
la qual le fue otorgada
con plenaria indulgençia,
y con tan mucha clemençia
que otra tal nunca fue dada.

112   Alto Rey: sacó las cruzes
y sus muy rricos pendones
con castillos y leones
a los canpos andaluzes;
por vengarse de marfuzes,
moros perros descreydos,
ca estauan engreydos
con espadas y capuzes.

113   Ally fueron con su seña
Aragon y Barçelona;
ally fueron de Panplona,
de Nauarra y de Gascueña;

ally fueron de Borgoña,
Portogal y Oliuençia;
acy fueron de Florençia,
infançones de Armeña.

114   Alli fueron dominantes
y del Papa sus legados;
alli fueron arreados
cardenales muy costantes;
ally fueron almirantes
y muy nobles arçobispos;
allý fueron con obispos
otros muchos batallantes.

115   Ally fueron de lonbardos
muy gentiles senescales;
ally fueron mariscales
de las Françias y picardos;
ally fueron muchos sardos
y tudescos y albanezes;
allí fueron marsellezes,
legitimos y bastardos.

116   Ally fueron con rromanos
grandes duques, altos condes;
alli fueron los viscondes
de Gerona y Pavidoanos;
ally füeron getanos
y muchos otros lenguajes;
alli fueron lindos pajes
con arcos ytalianos.

117   Ally fue la grant batalla
de las Nauas de Tolosa;
alli fue la espantosa
mortandat que no se calla;
ally fue vençido Abdalla,
el grant Miramamolin;
de ally fue como rruyn
fuyendo segund se falla.

117b. Navas de Tolosa: battle of 1212 which was quite important to the Reconquest, since the Moors were defeated there.

118 Ally fue mucho llamado
el Apostol Santïago;
ally fue dia aziago
para el pueblo rrenegado;
ally fue canonizado
el Rey Santo que diuiso;
ally fue su parayso:
aqui çierro mi cantado.

119 Alto Rey: sy bien notastes
estas cosas rrecontadas,
como van por sus pisadas
pocas menos vos pasastes;
ca, Señor, tanbien quedastes
de dos años en la cuna
quando començó Fortuna
en los rreynos que heredastes.

120 Alto Rey: ca estando ledo
vuestro padre en trono alto
por que yua dar vn salto
en los moros con denuedo;
salteóle muy sin miedo
la muerte crüel ladrona,
que a ninguno que perdona,
y matólo en Toledo.

121 11r Alto Rey: aquel costante
que fizo en su moçedad,
vos estando en la çibdad
de Segouia en este estante;
ordenó qu'el noble Infante
don Fernando, su hermano,
y la Reyna bien en llano
los rregiesen con talante.

122 Alto Rey: muy noblesçido
d'estos dos vuestros tutores
y muy nobles rregidores
fuestes vos bien nodresçido,

120b. "Vuestro padre": Enrique III, King of Castilla, 1379-1406.
121f. Don Fernando de Antequera, who later became Fernando I of Aragon.
121g. Reyna: Catalina, mother of Juan II of Castilla.

bien criado y guarnesçido
de costunbres muy rreales;
ca vos fueron tal leales
como fue bien paresçido.

123   Alto Rey: la noble cara,
vuestra madre y rregidora,
y el Infante sin demora
fueronse a Guadalfajara;
como quier que el rrey dexara
ordenado por sentençia
que vos diesen en tenençia
a dos grandes que el nonbrara.

124   Alto Rey: ardió la tea
en vuestra corte y mesnada,
fue la villa aluorosçada
y rrebuelta grant pelea
tan cruel y tanto fea,
que si Dios non acorriera
muy en breue ayna fuera
como chusma de Galea.

125   Alto Rey: fue amansado
el rrüydo con maneras
como quier que las denteras
non sallieron mal pecado;
por lo qual fue acordado
que todos de ally salliesen
y avn vos desque partiesen,
que seria todo allanado.

126   Alto Rey: luego partiestes
con la rreyna vna mañana
a Valladolid la llana
con grant gente que troxistes;
y desque ende vos metistes
duró diez años continnos
que solamente los caminos
a los ver nunca sallistes.

123h. "Dos grandes": King Enrique III had originally intended that Diego López de Estúñiga and Juan de Velasco have custody of the child.

127
Alto Rey: mucho preçiado
mas que oro nin que plata,
como leche solo nata,
ella vos touo guardado;
vuestro rreyno es ygualado,
veno la muerte rrauiosa
con su flecha poçoniosa
y matóla sin su grado.

128
Alto Rey: desque finada
la muy alta noblesçida,
fue la gente entristesçida
por su muerte y turbada;
enpero desque enterrada
luego en punto caualgastes
por la villa y rremirastes
vuestra corte muy onrrada.

129
Alto Rey: con grand ardid
fue por todos ordenado
qu'el noble Juan Furtado
fuese estonçe adalid;
el qual dixo: "Señor, yd
d'esta villa y miraredes
vuestro rreyno y folgaredes
en la villa de Madrid."

130
Alto Rey: desque llegada
vuestra corte y grandes onbres
que non digo aqui sus nonbres,
a la villa ya nonbrada
onde vos fue otorgada
la carga del rregimiento,
por cortes aconplimiento
de vuestra hedad acabada.

131 *11v*
Alto Rey: los aderentes
que estonçes vos aguardauan
por quitar muchos esgonçes
y peligros y açidentes,
por algunos continentes

127f-h. Queen Catalina died in 1418.
129c. Juan Furtado: nobleman of the court of Juan II.

que entre ellos se vsaron,
a Segouia vos tornaron
bien guardado con seruientes.

132   Alto Rey: los sus parientes
que con vos entraron dentro
non quesieron en su çentro
acoger mas infançones;
por lo qual los coscorrones
ayna fueron buscados,
ca fueron medio trabados
todos por los cabeçones.

133   Alto Rey: en la posada
del vuestro grant mayordomo,
Juan Furtado, que es en somo
de la calle enpedregada,
rrica fiesta vos fue dada
de famoso y grant convite,
mas pegaron vn enbite
los de fuera y cantonada.

134   Alto Rey: ca los tomaron
libremente en su poder
y a su guisa y plazer
de Segouia vos sacaron;
los de dentro se quedaron
escarnidos y burlados,
y del juego desuañados
y a su culpa se tornaron.

135   Alto Rey: a la parada
que de suso se rrepite
rribaron tal rrebite
los de dentro con çelada;
ca en vna trasnochada
dieron salto en Tordesillas
los qual fue mal y cosquillas
d'esta guerra començada.

136   Alto Rey: ca fue entrada
la vuestra muy rreal casa,
por lo qual mucha debrasa
ençendió esa caualgada,

la qual non es apagada;
quiera Dios que se apague
sin que mas pesares trague
Castilla la Trabajada.

137   Alto Rey: esto pasado,
luego dende a pocos dias
sin auer muchas porfias
vos, Señor, fuestes leuado
y non mucho a vuestro grado
a la çibdad entorrada,
Avila, la bien çercada,
do estouistes trabajado.

138   Alto Rey: ca se apartaron
los Infantes en dos partes,
sus banderas estandartes
en dos bandos se mostraron;
los del vno se ençerraron,
estouieron a pie quedo;
los del otro en Olmedo
grandes gentes ayuntaron.

139   Alto Rey: por las quistiones
ser terribles y dañosas
y por ser muy criminosas
entre si las diuisiones,
por quitar las ocasiones
rreboluieron su minera
y fueronse a Talauera
con banderas a montones.

140   Alto Rey: en esa villa
bien çercada de alto muro,
vos estando muy seguro
con vuestra rrica familia
... ...
que a sayo algund lacayo
vna cosa cuyda el bayo,
otra cuyda el que lo ensilla.

138b. The Infantes don Juan (later King of Navarra and Aragon), and don Enrique, Maestre of Santiago, sons of Fernando I of Aragon.

141   *12r*   Alto Rey: bien rrechaçar
en el juego de la pelota
aprouecha mas quien nota:
aqui va vn buen picar;
non vos sopieron guardar
los patrones que guardauan
pues cuydado ....
al se fize al mudrugar.

142   Alto Rey: muy rredotable
con esfuerço y atreuimiento,
lealtança y sentimiento
de amor muy entrañable,
vuestro leal conde estable
con sus armas de la Luna,
madrugó sin gente alguna
fizo fecho muy notable.

143   Alto Rey: Señor, notad
lo que fizo el leal conde
por ser cosa que rresponde
a grandeza y lealtad:
vos lançó en vn castillo
y guardó bien el pestillo
sin temor con onbredad.

144   Alto Rey: en Montaluan
es la torre en que estouiestes,
en la qual, Señor, sofriestes
grand trabajo y mucho afan;
ca por mengua de auer pan
vos dieron comer cauallos
vuestros leales vasallos,
a pesar de Sant Julian.

145   Alto Rey: fuestes velado
nüeue dias por cuenta
do pasaron grant tormenta
los de fuera en despoblado,
de mal tienpo agrauiado
que fazia de aguas y frios

142e, f. The *Condestable* of Castilla and favorite of King Juan II, Alvaro de Luna.

por cresçer tanto los rrios
qu'ellas non fallaron vado.

146   Alto Rey: çient mill tenblores
los de dentro alli pasaron,
ca por vos se auenturaron
a la muerte y sus pauores;
non les fallesçió rrencores
en pasar tan fuerte trago
como aquel que de hondo lago
con sospiros y subdores.

147   Alto Rey: sin mas tardar
los de fuera derramaron,
los de dentro vos sacaron
sano y libre y sin pesar;
pues de ally deuen contar
que estouiestes libre y suelto,
sin enbargo, y desenbuelto
como rrey para mandar.

148   Alto Rey: luego folgastes
con los vuestros y rreystes
y despues que de ally salistes
vuestros rreynos ordenastes;
asoluistes, condenastes,
como rrey y grant señor,
sin rreçelo y sin temor
de algunos que desterrastes.

149   Alto Rey: y avn ygualastes
a los grandes y a los chicos,
a los pobres y a los rricos,
ca todos los perdonastes;
por lo qual, Señor, quitastes
del rreyno todas las rraças
y por mercados y plaças
pregonar lo mandastes.

150   Alto Rey: las otras cosas
que en vuestro rreyno pasaron,
pues que todos las miraron
non cunple rrezar mas prosas;
ca serien muy enojosas

si todas se rrepitiesen,
y creo que non copiesen
en muchos testos y glosas.

151   *12v*   Alto Rey: pues rretornando
al proposito de ençima
que fundo en vna rrima,
por sus puntos va encaxando;
y por ende yd escuchando
lo que digo y propongo,
sin falaça y sin diptongo
mis dichos metrificando.

152   Alto Rey: si es mirado
mi proçeso bien de yuso,
fallarán en el incluso
asaz bïen declarado;
que vos fue bien perturbado
vuestro grand plazer y gloria
por quitarvos la vitoria
del buen fecho començado.

153   Alto Rey: ca ordenastes
de fazer guerra a los moros,
vos teniendo asas thesoros
para ello que ayuntastes;
mas luego que començastes
para lo poner en obra,
rrecodió vos tal çoçobra
como al rrey de que escuchastes.

154   Alto Rey: ca manifiesto
es a todos vuestros grandes,
y lo saben los de Flandes
el fecho muy desonesto,
por entrar con brauo gesto
los rreys muy atreuidos,
con sus pendones ·tendidos
en Castilla con rrepuesto.

155   Alto Rey: a suelta rrienda
llegaron çerca de Fita,
mas su estança fue poquita
y voluieron sin contienda;

por lo qual esta fazienda
me paresçe fonda sima,
ca grant juego de esgrima
yo non sé quien lo entienda.

156   Alto Rey: vos los seguistes
en los sus rregnos entrando,
destruyendo y quemando
quanto vos por bien touistes;
mas despues non consentistes
vsando de la grandeza,
que feziesen mas crüeza
y contento vos füestes.

157   Alto Rey: si bien mirades
este fuego ya ençendido,
tan cruel y tan cresçido,
fallaredes que oy estades
en tales nesçesidades
como estouo el rrey que cuento,
y por mas avisamiento
cunple que oyades.

158   Ca el rrey, doncas e çertas,
de Aragon y de Sesilla,
tener deue grant mansilla
por sus gentes presas y muertas;
por ver talar sus hüertas
non terná grant paçïençia,
quanto mas ver a Valençia
corrida fasta las puertas.

159   Pües, Señor, contenplad
en don Juan, Rey de Nauarra:
visto es que se socarra
la su tierra a mas andar;
cada qual puede pensar
su trabajo y su tristor
por auer tanto dolor
que terná muy grand pesar.

156a. Although the copyist wrote "Alto Rey: por los siguientes," it does not rhyme, and is probably an error. A possible alternative is offered here.

158a. Although the meaning of the initial words is not clear, it is obvious that Baena refers to Alfonso V of Aragon.

160   Pues, Señor, quien bien acata
los Infantes que padesçen
como quier que se bastesçen
Fortuna los desbarata,
son corridos fasta mata
de ser dentro en Alburquerque;
este fuego de alquerque
malo es sinon se amata.

161   *13r*   Pues, Señor, la vuestra hermana,
la Infante, está insegura,
sin plazer y sin folgura,
sospirando muy sin gana
por non ser tanto çercana
de vos, Rey, como solia;
por lo qual pidió valia
a su nieto de Santana.

162   Pues, Señor, ca Portugal
tiene cara con dos fazes,
ca profaza de los rrapases
sofismando logical;
que rremesçe el pertegal
el Infante don Düarte,
que anda con su arte
contra vos non leal.

163   Pues, Señor, los enemigos,
ynfieles moros perros,
que vos han fecho mill yerros
non serán vuestros amigos;
quanto mas que sin testigos
se prueua por esperiençia,
como son grand pestilençia
d'este rreyno muy contrarios.

164   Pues, Señor, en la montaña
de Castilla y su algarue
non fallesçe quien escarue
y quien sienbre gran sisaña;
ca muchos juegan de maña

160b. See 138b.
162f. Don Duarte of Portugal.

esta es la que mas quema,
cada qual tener su tema
de segar son su aguadaña.

165   Pues, Señor, abrid los ojos,
ca non cunple que dormades,
mas que luego proueades
arrancando estos abrojos;
sinon, canpos y rrestrojos
con las lanças son arados,
y de sangre bien rregados,
y con muertos y despojos.

166   Ca, Señor, sy non se apaga
este fuego con mucha agua
antes que arda mas la flama
nin se dañe aquesta llaga,
mas terrible es esta plaga
que la que padesçe Françia,
ca por guerra y distançia
todo su rreyno se estraga.

167   Y por ende, a tantos males
acorret con los rremedios,
pues tenedes muchos medios
y mengüas, Señor, tales,
que de viboras mortales
rresgalgar y de escurpiones,
sanarán sus corrupciones
pues qüantas y qüales.

168   Oh, Rey brauo, muy dorado
y de grand pres valioso,
sodes vos el Generoso
Alto Rey muy ylustrado;
y por sabios es fallado
esta ser mas noble espeçia
que en el mundo mucho presçia
todo monge y muy letrado.

169   La Infante muy preçiosa
y suaue oliente magna

_169a._ The Infanta, doña Isabel, daughter of Juan II.

es la noble y soberana
alta rreyna y poderosa,
tan discreta y tan fermosa
que su muy rreal senblante
de sanar esto es bastante
con su vista muy graçiosa.

170   La lançeta muy delgada
cria el angel vuestro fijo,
la qual tiene en condesijo
con el mesmo bien guardada;
el dará tal lançetada
y fará rreal sangria,
por que torná en alegria
a Castilla sin lançada.

171 13v   El almina consolante
que abrando la garganta
es la rreyna, buena, santa,
vuestra hermana enperante:
y la muy linda Infante
que rrelunbra como estrella,
es rrazon de ser con ella
muy fino dia gargante.

172   Los enplastos prouechosos
son los grandes caualleros
y leales consejeros
con buen seso estudiosos;
ca deuen ser acuçiosos
por seruiçio de Dios y vuestro,
que non tomen el seniestro
estos fechos peligrosos.

173   Los socroçios son pastores
y perlados de la Eglesia,
pues que saben la conseja
y los vuestros abditores;
y tan bien sabios doctores
de quien vos tanto fïades,
sy con saña porfïades
lean bien los rrelatores.

170b. His son, Enrique, who later became Enrique IV of Castilla.

174   Los vnguentos olïosos
y los blandos süaues,
estos tienen so las llaues
los muy buenos rreligiosos;
y ellos rreueguen muy llorosos
con ayuno y oraçiones,
que Dios alçe execuçiones
d'estos fechos criminosos.

175   Los manjares y dïetas
non serán solos garuanços,
nin capones nin betanços,
nin lauancos, nin çerçetas,
mas personas muy discretas,
de nobles enbaxadores
y leales tratadores
y mas sabios que profetas.

176   El agua dulçe tenprada
en que vañen al paçiente
non será del agua ardiente
nin tanpoco agua rrosada,
mas será agua llorada
de gemidos y de los pobres,
ca batiéndose estos cobres
toda la tierra es talada.

177   El açucar conortoso
non será de los rrosado,
nin tan poco violado
nin de pan maguer sabroso,
mas será mas glorïoso
que la paz y la concordia,
y quitada la discordia
todo el rreyno es gososo.

178   Oh grant fisico prudente
que ha de dar aqui consuelo,
este solo está en el çielo
en su trono exçelente;
y si El pone el vnguente
con la su mano bendita,

el enfermo y su pepita
es librado en continente.

179   Boticario muy çertero
mucho cunple que se busque
por Castilla y se rrebusque
muy fïel y verdadero,
por que todo el bien entero
del enfermo su beuir,
del sanar y del morir
todo va en el espeçiero.

180   Ca, Señor, por su çedaço
las mengüas con coladas,
y por el son destenpladas
y meçidas con su braço;
pero guarden que su caço
non sea palo d'adelfa,
en disiendo que es d'arquelfa
a muy muchos dan del maço.

181 *14r*   Por lo qual muy apurado
deue ser tal ofiçial
y mas claro qu'el cristal
para fecho tan granado;
y por ser bien atenprado
el xarope y non amargo,
Señor, tome este cargo
el vuestro leal priuado.

182   Ca es noble y poderoso,
muy ardid y esforçado,
muy cortes y mesurado,
y gentil y muy graçioso,
sobre todo venturoso;
por lo qual el lo meresçe
y a el solo pertenesçe
este ofiçio tan famoso.

183   Por seys cosas señaladas
qu'el guardó muy prouechosas,
tan leales y famosas

181h. "Leal priuado": Alvaro de Luna.

que debien ser coronadas
de uos, Rey, y muy loadas;
las quales, Señor, son estas
que serán de yuso puestas
por mi lengua publicadas.

184 La primera: la persona
vos guardó con amor fuerte
y se puso a la muerte
muchas vezes del azcona.
La segunda es grand corona
que vos dio el alta fama
pues guardó la rreal cama
de las damas la corona.

185 La terçera: la espada
vos guardó muy sin maliçia,
ca tiró de uos codiçia
de tenerla ensangrentada.
La qüarta: fue guardada
la pendola sin engaño,
ca por el en vuestro daño
nunca distes pendolada.

186 La quinta es la mesura
qu'el guardó y vos vsastes,
ca nunca deseredastes
a ninguno por trauesura.
La sesta es grant cordura
qu'el guardó por vias buenas,
ca, Señor, vuestras almenas
non las distes con soltura.

187 Por la qual grant lealtança
qu'el guardó tan lealmente
es y fue bien meresçiente
de durar en su priuança;
y avn deue auer fiança
de pujar de grado en grado
y cobrar mayor estado
pües vos fue sin errança.

188   Y pues el touo tenprança
tanto tienpo con buen seso,
y guardó derecho el peso
y muy justa la balança,
en juntar paz y amistança,
en mesclar este xarope
a que Dios queriendo tope
el terná tal ordenança.

189   Alto Rey? maguer non cabe
de loar su nobleza,
su ardid y gentileza
todo el rreyno bien lo sabe;
y avn que yo non lo alabe,
los sus fechos lo alaban
ca los nobles non acaban
de loar lo que en el cabe.

190   Alto Rey: vuestro palaçio
cria muchos sabidores
que se preçian de amores
y son de grant generaçio;
si quitar quieren profaçio
de caer en lenguas malas
y volar con rricas alas,
noten este bien despaçio.

191 *14v*   Alto Rey: de tranco en tranco
y pasado por los fechos
breuemente por sus fechos
cada cosa por su blanco;
ca, Señor, Alto Rey franco,
concluyendo mi rrescrito,
pues ando çerca del fito,
quiero dar dentro en el blanco.

192   Alto Rey: bien por menudo
he contado la biuienda
del buen rrey y la emienda
que buscó como sesudo;

---

188. The order of these lines in the manuscript is a, b, c, d, f, g, e, h, but has been changed here to preserve the rhyme scheme.

por su seso y dotrina
dio salud y melezina
a su rreyno segunt cudo.

193   Alto Rey: asy acorra
la vuestra merçet en breue,
con rremedios segunt deue
al doliente sin engorra,
por que non dé con su porra
al diablo a sobre vienta,
ca mal quema su pemienta
al que duerme a la modorra.

194   Alto Rey: pues entendedes
mi sermon, lo que declina,
mucho en breue y muy ayna
bien será que escutedes;
lo que fizo vos sabedes,
el Rey Santo y Bendicho
don Alfonso, el sobre dicho,
lo qual fecho folgaredes.

195   Alto Rey: ca vuestro abuelo
ayuntó a vuestro padre
con la rreyna vuestra madre,
y metiólo so vn velo
por sanar el gran rreçelo
del grant Duque de Alencastre
qu'el ganara por deslastre
este rreyno muy sin duelo.

196   Alto Rey: aqui va el pique
de quitar estos agrazes,
de juntar aquestas pazes
para sienpre sin rreplique;
todo el rreyno vos suplique
a que dé muy rricas arras
a la flor de la nauarras,
vuestro fijo, don Enrrique.

197   Alto Rey: luego es quitada
toda la vmor y flema

195a. His grandfather, Enrique II, King of Castilla from 1333-1379.

y la sangre y la postema
luego es clarificada;
y la rret que está armada
con los lazos del diablo,
sin mas armas nin venablo
d'esta será rregistrada.

198   Alto Rey: luego es sano
el doliente sin dubdança,
y vibra en grant folgança
el buen rreyno castellano;
pues, Señor, luego tenprano
acorred pues que podedes,
y fased lo que deuedes
como rrey fiel cristïano.

199   Alto Rey: y sea dada
sentençia difinitiua,
muy rreal consolatiua
por vuestra boca rrezada;
la qual sea coronada,
bien escrita en letras de oro,
por quitar tristeza y lloro
d'esta guisa executada.

200   Alto Rey: vos perdonando
a los rreys por nobleza
y vsando de rrealeza
los Infantes rreleuando,
otros grandes non matando,
oluidando sus errores,
a los otros mas menores
con flanqueza algo les dando.

201   *15r*   Alto Rey: y por los buenos
y seruiçios señalados
que su padre fizo loados
de grant lealtança llenos,
ca destruyó los agarenos
y las sus muy viles setas,
y mamándovos las tetas
ensanchó los vuestros rreynos.

202   Alto Rey: ca en la frontera
vos ganó las tierras nueuas,
Santa, Pligo, y las cueuas
y Cañete y Aznalmera,
y subió vuestra bandera
en la torre del Alhaquin
y ganó del Rey Ozmin
Xebar, Huete, Antequera.

203   Alto Rey: por contenplança
del rrey noble, vuestro tio,
que ganó tanto gentio
de los moros por su lança,
dignos son de perdonança
los fijos d'esta falda,
quanto mas la sangre alta
que non piden mas vengança.

204   Alto Rey: asas abasta
la vengança ya tomada,
pues de todo está follada
la su tierra que lo lasta;
y, Señor, tanbien se gasta
de la vuestra grant partida,
por lo qual agua vertida
mal se coje con canasta.

205   Alto Rey: por ende çese
vuestra grant saña y ablande
por que el diablo non ande
mas ordiendo y se rremese;
ca, Señor, sy Dios quesiese
dar sosiego y mucha paz
y concordia y grant solaz,
esto es vuestro interese.

206   Alto Rey: maguer non quepa
en mi seso atal espejo
que los deua dar consejo,
la vuestra merçed lo sepa;

202f. Alhaquin (Alhakem) caliph of Cordoba.
203b. "Vuestro tio": Fernando I of Aragon.

que mirando bien la çepa
donde vos y ellos venides,
çesarán todas las lides
y los daños d'esta tropa.

207   Cesarán luego conbates
por la mar y por la tierra;
çesará la crüel guerra
y los muy grandes debates;
çesarán muchos deslates
de truenos y de ballestas;
çesarán todas rrequestas,
pleÿtos y calcofates.

208   Cesarán los carracones,
carracas, naos, galeas;
çesarán crudas peleas,
contiendas y disensiones;
çesarán venir questiones
de los rreynos estrangeros;
çesarán de gastar dineros;
folgarán los coraçones.

209   Cesarán los capitanes
de los muy nobles françeses;
çesarán los genoueses
y bretones y alimanes;
çesarán los sacomanes
de rapinas y garueos;
çesarán grandes arreos
de Milan y Jasojarnes.

210   Cesarán venir plumajes
de otras muchas naçiones;
çesarán las rrendiçiones
de los presos y de los gajes;
çesarán grandes parajes
de estrangeros por los puertos;
çesarán de non ser muertos
en Castilla asas linaje.

211 *15v*   Cesarán los rrobadores
y verán mundo rrebuelto;
çesarán rrio büelto

ganançia de pescadores;
çesarán los matadores
temiendo vuestra presençia;
çesarán mal y dolençia
y beuirán los pecadores.

212   Cesarán luego monedas,
los pedidos y cohechos;
çesarán los otros pechos,
folgarán las gentes ledas;
çesarán y estarán quedas
las villas y los solares;
çesarán muchos forçares
por caminos y veredas.

213   Cesarán carros carretas
de andar por los caminos;
çesarán a los mesquinos
los males d'estas saetas;
çesarán muchos profetas
de Merlin y Rocaçisa;
çesarán por esta guisa
atables y tronpetas.

214   Cesarán luego traydores
que texen falsa tela;
çesarán fuego y candela
y malos caçadores;
çesarán rrevoluedores,
falsarios y desleales;
çesarán todos los males
a pesar de mezcladores.

215   Cesarán todos los plantos
de pobres y doloridos;
çesarán grandes gemidos
y sus lloros y quebrantos;
çesarán luego los plantos
de todos los que padesçen;
çesarán quantos meresçen
que tengan de uos espantos.

213f. Rocaçisa: Rocacelsa, a monk of Montserrat of the fourteenth century, gifted with prophecy.

216   Cesarán persecuçiones
y sospiros de las gentes;
çesarán entre sus dientes
que non lançen maldeçiones;
çesarán tribulaçiones,
rrogarán por vuestra vida;
çesará de ser corrida
la Eglesia y sus perdones.

217   Cesarán portogaleses
y todos los sus gauarros;
çesarán tanbien nauarros,
eso mesmo los ingleses;
çesarán aragoneses
y todos los omesillos;
quedarán para morillos
malos años, negros meses.

218   Alto Rey: por que vos rruego,
con la Virgen Santa Maria,
que vuestra grant señoria
rremate todo este fuego,
y que sea fecho luego
antes que entren los veranos,
y sinon, lauo mis manos
y alço mano del juego.

219   Alto Rey: mi artefiçio
que va escrito en pergamino
y vos declaro buen camino
para vos beuir en viçio
luengos tienpos sin bulliçio;
y, Señor, d'esto que digo
a Dios tomo por testigo,
pues que vuestro bien codiçio.

                Ffenida

220   Alto Rey: fin del arenga.
Dios del çielo vos mantenga,
y vos guarde y vos sostenga,
y vuestra merçet me tenga
mis trabajos en seruiçio.

---

219. The order of these verses in the manuscript is a, b, d, e, f, g, h, c, but has been corrected here to coincide with the established rhyme scheme.

TRANSLATION

1. To so excellent a king belongs such a gift.

2. Eminent, sovereign King of the kingdoms of Castilla, seated, as noble royalty should, upon your throne: please accept this pleasant work which I, your servant, offer to you, with my good intentions.

3. If you read this well and take note of my process, you will not see one excess in the verse form; and I believe that you will enjoy it, for through it your present worries will be alleviated.

4. According to the worthy Bartolo, those who protest are quite excellent: and so I protest here at the beginning, in poetry, for I will write all of this about the kings and the *Infantes*.

5. I surrender myself, therefore, to your protection and mercy, since what I will say is for your just service; here lies a great secret: whoever rigidly quiets his king does not do well at all.

6. Although in Deza they have the custom of beating him that blunders, and also here in Baeza they use other means to quiet him who speaks the truth, since they break his head.

7. Praised Sir: although I certainly know that they will split my head for having written this treatise, and though I know I will be burned like blazing kindling, I will never be a coward, for I am proven loyal to you.

8. For I am writing this to serve these noblemen, and also for the honor and advantage of your kingdom; so, excellent king, if you recognize this I am sure that you will gladly show me mercy.

9. I beg and plead of the noblemen, the good *fidalgos* of selected lineage, that they not forget what I write, for good intentions and not bad are included in it.

10. Although I may be defeated by the envious, damning arguers, I nevertheless present my work; but I swear on the Lord that such an opus was never seen in Spain.

11. So listen lords, *infantes,* and prelates; dukes, counts, *adelantados,* teachers and priors, marshals, magistrates of cities and towns; may all hear these wonders, and may the poets not be alarmed.

12. So listen Castilians, great sages of Ramon Llull and clever alchemists, and dull townsmen, Jews, Moors, Christians, friars, monks, laymen, cripples, maimed ones, blindmen; scribes, prepare your pens.

13. And may the followers of this art of poetry re-examine each point of the stroke of their pen, without having their eyes filled with cobwebs; and may the great sophisters take note of any fallacy, for I hope to write this without errors.

14. Although I am a bad chronicler, I did read page for page the famous and great conquest of the city of Troy; and also the Roman chronicle of the gentiles; and the clever, three-part, Italian stories.

15. I read well the great, the subtle *Old Testament* of the old and the new law, which is so deep a cave, I do not know who can understand it.

16. I read Vegecius who wrote about battles and who knew how to depict them and put them in great esteem; I read Titus Livius, Boethius, Seneca, and Lucan; I did not read these books I describe like a fool.

17. I read Cato, and the learned poet Dante, Ovid the Inspiring, Virgil, Plato, Ramon Llull, Homer Novato, Rogel and Policrates, Ricardo and Celon.

18. I read the moral works of Aristotle the Wise, the battles of Strabo, Euclid, and Natales; and I read the stories that Boccaccio tells; I read the philosophical books of Macrobius and Horace.

19. I read the great poets, and Cicero and Tiberius, Zarquel and Valerius, and other readings on the sun and planets and the brilliant rays, bright and flashing, of the stars and the comets.

20. I read the logical cadences, the liberal arts, prose, songs, and the Latin works of the Limousines; and I read the *saradines* that Rome, the guide, composed, and I read of the mountains of Turkey in Florentine songs.

21. I read the perfect *Partidas* and *Ordenamientos* and the *Fueros* and *Regimientos* and the total of Ambrose; I also read of the Law of Bartolo and the books that deal in depth with the frightening sciences, and of the rock of Cumas where Sybil lived.

22. I read in Baena, where I learned to make drafts and eat capers at supper; and I read the books of Avicena and his just ideas; Eminent King: my silogisms are ending, but something else is sounding.

23. I read in the histories of many tournaments that Moses and his Hebrews won; I read of Judas and the Macabeans, and of the just and great man, Joshua, and even of Samson who killed the Philistines.

24. I read that Gideon fought in such great conflicts that they caused the crude deaths of the Pharoah's men; Saul, Solomon, and King David, who saw his good son Absalon killed in battle.

25. I read of the dominion of the great King Alexander, according to Saint Leander, who defeated the power of King Dario with his force, and who conquered the whole world, land and sea and its depths, saying: "All is mine."

26. I read, with great desire, of the mortal field battles that Caesar and Pompey had; of King Ptolemy, and Hannibal the African, of Scipio, and of Trajan I read great things.

27. I read of the frightening and cruel war of Troy, where so many riches and people were lost; and the venerable, powerful King Priam died, along with both his sons, Paris and Hector, the Notable.

28. I read, but with great sorrow, that once this great king was dead, they very wrongfully killed his daughter, Polyxena. May you be damned, Helen, with all your beauty, for you caused such sadness, and did not act as a good woman!

29. I read that the city was razed to the ground, and there was much grief when they saw that the beautiful lover of Achilles was kidnapped, and was beheaded by the cruel hands of Pyrrhus.

30. I read many ugly things about the loss of Troy, all done by Eneas in great Illion, for Menalaus sold the Palladium to the Greeks; when he saw Helen in the ship he raised sails abruptly.

31. I read of the Captain and Duke of Bouillon; of Narcissus and Jason, of Hercules and Roland, Charlemagne and Florestan, of Amadis and Lancelot, Valdovin and Camelot, of Galas and Tristan.

32. I read of Tamerlaine, who was much greater than Constantine, or Marcus or Latino, or even Presbiter John; and I read of the great sultan and of the strong Morato, and of others I do not describe, who came after Adam.

33. I read of all those great men, of Count Fernan Gonzalez, of the good Cid and of other such men who destroyed many lands to prevent the Goths from winning in ancient times; and I read of King Roderic many things.

34. I read that the kings of Spain did great deeds while warring, conquering many lands; I speak of some of these kings in short, since my pens is becoming angry from writing.

35. I do want to say that I read of the nobility of two kings who had noble laws and did deeds of wonder; Fernando and his men who won many goods from the noble cities of Cordoba and Sevilla.

36. Although in summary, I read of Algeciras and its governor, of Alcala de Aben-Zaide which was won by the good warrior Alfonso the Last; for thusly he was named, and he was the gentlest man born after Nero.

37. I read in shortened form of some predecessors who were emperors (but I'll not go on naming them), from the great don Fernando to the great conqueror, grandson of the emperor, don Alfonso, omitting other names.

38. I end here my poetic work, for I did not want to go on telling of others; but it is wrong to be silent about the deeds done by the kings who followed him.

39. I am now tired and my tongue is also tiring, although I was a coward and deserved to be blamed because I did not tell of the other famous kings, those glorious saints, but I hope to be pardoned for it.

40. For I did not write this to waste paper nor ink, nor for deceit, since I did not read these things quickly; but I should not name more of these men without also mentioning other related situations.

41. I have singed my eyebrows from reading so much, which is reason enough to conclude my stories; so may the ears of all who love you listen, and they will see that I should not be called a dumb peasant.

42. According to rumor, your kingdom is ailing from such a great misfortune that it is burning like a flame; and so it cries out from the pain and has complained of a toothache for days.

43. It was not purged as it should have been, nor cured in the manner that should have been required, so it remained sick and full of humors that give it great tremblings and pains in the side.

44. The fever of Palenzuela was gone, but the affliction continued, so the fever returned; may God protect it from the ague so that its destruction may not come, and that it may enjoy warmth daily.

45. Aside from the fever, there are other certain signs of sickness which are hidden, but already lodged in its kidneys; and its lungs are swollen and even palsy if feared, and if the dropsy grows on, it is a sure sign of hopelessness.

46. Its ardors and severe pains become more alive each day, and even worse; and it cries out so loudly in its pain that Popes, kings, and emperors feel badly about it.

47. If the wise and discrete teachers do not help it, the humor will worsen; for, my Lord, according to my own conjecture, this evil comes from afar.

48. Some loyal, undeceptive plasters were needed for the damages of these wars and struggles, the great evils and great losses begun with mockery, and for the tumbles and the crude business.

49. Also needed are medicines made of syrup and new wine, rhubarb syrup, and a lot of other fine antidotes; in addition to sugary sauces, it should also eat good food and put soothing balms where the thorns are.

50. Other cures are plasters for the spine which chill more than lead, and other cold treatments; also good bleedings, but above all some baths of sweet water made from sugar cane so that the sourness of the disease comes out.

51. A great physician is needed to order the purges; also fire and carbon and a wise pharmacist, a very clever herbalist, who could make the concoctions.

52. So if you want to cure these ills without doctors, sciences, nor expenditures, my Lord, you should take note of my response, and what King Alfonso did, you also will do.

53. It is not found in writing or in law that in the world there ever was a king so fortunate for such a long time, nor conquered by so many; however, although defeated, he was well aided by God, and was not helpless.

54. According to what they say, he was the grandson of the discrete emperor, the famed don Alfonso; and he was the son of the honored King Sancho whom they adored, and everyone called him the Beloved Saint King.

55. He was a small child, a tot of only four years and very lovely and blessed; the vile, damned devil began to arm his battle of evil and envy in the manner which I will repeat.

56. It was advised to his uncle, don Fernando the Villain, King of Leon, that the child's united kingdom be destroyed through Castilla, and that they rob everything they might find in the fields and in the towns.

57. The young king was advised of the false ruins and they irritated him so, that he believed the troublemakers; he did so for two reasons: so that the kingdom might not be lost, and afterwards he recovered a lot of money without much ado.

58. It was so done without delay, for his uncle, the ready king, worked with great greed, fearlessly and without conscience to dig into the towns and castles of the child-king.

59. Because of these evils that Castilla suffered because of the uncle, there arose a great quarrel among the loyal servants; they fought without daggers in order to find out to which official the custody and upbringing of the child-king would be given.

60. And it was given to Gutierre de Castro, but he was so badly defeated that they took the task away from him; and the child was then given to the great count, don Enrique, about whom there is such great controversy, that I am afraid.

61. Then that child was given to Garcia de Daza, a very unfortunate man; and because of this the Castros and Laras broke many weapons over who would take the state.

62.   Don Enrique feared very much that these things would be very dangerous, for don Fernando was coming to see the king; so waiting and sleeping he would kidnap the king and flee with him to Soria.

63.   The kingdom knew such storms that time that the total of its affronts were blacker than a fish; the twelve-year old king took all the tithes, and without accounting, cast many people from their protection.

64.   In the reading about this persecuted child it is thoroughly recounted that he had great luck; and don Enrique complained so much that, although he was a nobleman, he consented that if they gave him something, he would promise to hand over the child.

65.   Thusly accused, don Enrique, who was awarded with the child-king, arose at a bad time and made a bargain that the child-king kiss the hand of his uncle and give him servitude.

66.   Then the cruel king, and don Manrique with him, left for Soria, because don Enrique had promised this; and as soon as he arrived there he demanded that the child give him the agreement he had sworn, so that it might be fulfilled.

67.   Those who were guarding the child, who was in dismay in the arms of his guardian, all cried before him; and lamenting and sighing for that perfidy and bad bargain that dealt with the child-king.

68.   All said: "O Blessed Saint Mary, such error and evil no one has ever seen; they gave the king to us freely, and now to you, Count, we deliver him." And they dismissed themselves from the king.

69.   Then a nobleman, a good vassal, mounted a horse and did a cunning deed: he stole the child without delay and hid him under a cape, running hastily to Gormaz, the fortress.

70.   Since the child did not give servitude and did not leave with him, his bad uncle made a great fuss and cursed; and with anger he turned to the brave count to collect the bargain and oath, since the child did not deliver.

71.   The crude king was delayed by making sure that the child was asleep; but a short time later he was told that a man had come there and must have fled with the child.

72.   The very irate uncle then regretted that the child was stolen, and he became faint because he was badly ridiculed by the count and his promise; and a great fuss was raised in Soria.

73.   Then the tyrannical king left unhappily, since the sprightly child-king had escaped and was free; he was very angry and still protesting, so everyone searched for the child day and night.

74. The two brothers of the good count searched so they were found clean of guilt; the loyal Count Nuño travelled hills and plains until he found the child among peasants.

75. Without much trouble he came upon him in Atienza; fearlessly and shamelessly he conveyed that his family was saved by this deed from the bad bargain and from ruin, for he freed the child from the power of the savage king.

76. Then a demand was made of don Manrique by the king (which was more of a threat than a demand), that he come to answer about the lie, and he perjured that the battle was ready.

77. Don Manrique was proud in answering and defending his honor, and said angrily to the king: "I was not nor am I treacherous, nor a traitor, nor liar, but I deserve to be taken for loyal and great."

78. It was then determined by judgement that don Manrique did not lie nor was wronged; and it was determined that he freed his king from servitude and gave him splendor, and should be crowned.

79. Once don Manrique was freed from this trouble, another undertaking of the wronged child-king arose; soon he was a young man and he worked hard for his honor and was avenged of those who wronged him.

80. The good child, the gentle Alfonso, who was esteemed by one hundred thousand, then travelled throughout his kingdom, not hunting falcons, but seeking the thieves, and frightening more than thunder.

81. The great suffering and sadness he knew because of the robbery and tyranny of his uncle put him in a difficult situation, like a bull in a ring which is run and speared.

82. So very angrily and with fitful signs he ruined the kings, his relatives, without order; whoever tasted the sauce and wasted his kingdom paid the due price after he ate.

83. First he began his task by avenging himself openly of his uncle the unjust ruler; like a just king he chased him for the robbery and the barter that the old runner had done to him.

84. Then he defeated him many times in the fields and brought him to the dregs of life, alone, without his men; he finally conquered him and took his land from him, then without delay chased him till he was dead.

85. Once his evil uncle was killed, Alfonso did not forget his cousin the inheritor; he quickly spurred on and chased him, tearing his cloak and leaving him dishonored.

86. Once the father, son, and their men were sought out, dishonored, and lost and cast from their kingdoms of Navarra, he chased King Sancho, who had a wide kingdom of ill-gained lands.

87. Thus travelling, this strong and brave child did not give any credit to those who had wronged him; nor did he leave Aragon without its due, for he destroyed its king with his great band of men.

88. Portugal was very rash and dissembled, and although it had much grandeur because it was very rich, this daring king chased them through the fields and left them quite wretched, sad, and suffering.

89. Once his enemies were thusly destroyed, he began to make attacks against the renegades, those false Moors, and soon he won from them Cuenca and the meadows of Yberlenca, which today are closed towns.

90. Once this child saw himself wounding and feasting on the Moors, and saw himself brave and feared, he gave out a great cry to gain honor and glory, and swore that his name would reach even Fez.

91. Since the king had a good heart and good intentions, for he wanted to serve God, in order to isolate the Moors, those dogs, he began to work hard and follow them with stubbornness.

92. He went to Alarcos with his men on horseback with bows, but went with bad luck; for one hundred thousand Moors came out from the lakes, and killing at any risk, so he left there without net nor ship.

93. Then destroyed, he was relentlessly chased five leagues by the Moors, and he was quite wounded; however, he was not taken by the Moors or warriors for he climbed a hill, where he received help.

94. He wanted very much to give the Moors a whipping and to turn swiftly from within and without, but with biting envy the neighboring kings, who were jealous and evil, blocked his passage.

95. Since this king and broken man was disoriented, they rose up against him; finding this a siutable occasion, a great throng of enemies fell onto him with such a great thud, all just to rid of him.

96. Soon Portugal raised its banner, threatening; his cousin, the King of Leon, rose up against him; King Sancho the Navarrese rose up with a bad motive; King Alfonso of Aragon arose with a great stoning.

97. From Granada arrived the Moorish king and the Berbers; from Alhamares many renegades came; another king with Saracens rose in mutiny; the whole sleepy land rose up, swarming with sailors.

98. From the pagans another king of the Alarabs emerged; Comenzarabs, the Turkish king, and spies rose up; of the Africans came a leader of the Almohardes; generals more dense than Milanese came also.

99. In his kingdom there emerged plenty of parasites; there arrived scoundrels of the jails of the abyss; in Christianity there arose against him so many contraries that they could not be counted by the account of Arab codes.

100. Since this king was surrounded by such great enemies as I have recounted above, he could not take pleasure with such sadness and great worry; he did not know what to do, since he believed he was alone.

101. This king thought he had good advice and accord, like any sane man, with the queen, his wife; he also wanted to know what advice his men who loved him would give him in his great need.

102. This king did not find any protection nor other aid to help his worries and complaints, except for the one I will explain, which was to give his lovely daughter in marriage to his cousin, the King of Leon.

103. They joined the two lovers immediately, and married them with a thousand jousts and drums; the noble, valiant king made all things equal, and once the royal wedding was over, they lived as they pleased.

104. This accomplished, they became quite equal: father-in-law and son-in-law were very happy and all the strife was removed; the noble king willingly returned all the territory he had taken from his son-in-law.

105. The people were sad because they saw father-in-law and son-in-law so close in desires, for they saw themselves unfortunate because the king would turn from them only to run and squeeze them as he had done before.

106. In order that the negotiations might be forever secure like the strength of high walls, and so they would not be broken, they swore that they would keep only two points, that Castilla and Leon would be joined into one kingdom.

107. This king strangely acted more like a master, which I will show: he softened his anger and rancor, which always disturbs and harms; with the Moors he very skillfully made bargains, pacts, peace, and other oaths.

108. Once the treaties were firmly agreed, this king began to do great deeds in his kingdoms; in Burgos he gave donations to the poorhouses, which no other past king has done.

109. The familiar proverb says: "In each place and time, he who suffers misery, or he who lives with sin, never sleeps, but writes misery upon his heart."

110. Similarly, he never forgot for a moment the dishonor and destruction that he had known before; and seeing himself unhappy, defeated by the Moors, he was always disposed to avenge himself soon.

111. This king did a famous deed; he begged the Pope to call his cause a crusade, which was given him with plenary indulgence and with such clemency that no such other was ever given.

112. He took his crosses and his rich standards with castles and lions to the Andalusian lands to get revenge on the scoundrels, the Morrish, pagan dogs, for they were being vain with their swords and capes.

113. With his signal went men from Aragon and Barcelona; from Pamplona, Navarra and Gascoña men went there; they went from Burgundy, Portugal, Olivencia, Florence, and Armenia.

114. Dominant men and legates of the Pope went there, with very constant cardinals, admirals and noble archbishops, bishops, and many other warriors.

115. Very genteel nobles of Lombardy went there, with officials from France, and Picards, Sardinians, Germans, Albanians, Marseillians, legitimate sons and bastards.

116. Great dukes and eminent counts went there with Romans, as well as vicecounts of Gerona and Paduans, gypsies and others, and handsome pages with Italian bows.

117. The great battle of Navas of Tolosa took place there; there occurred many deaths which are well known; Abdalla, the great Miramamolin, was defeated there; from there he left ruined, fleeing, according to history.

118. The Apostle Saint James was often called upon there; it was a fatal day for the renegades; the Saint King that I describe was canonized there; there was his Paradise; here I close my song.

119. If you note well, eminent King, these deeds I have related, as they go step by step, few less have happened to you; for, my Lord, you also were but two years old in the cradle when Fortune began in the kingdom you inherited.

120. For your father was happy on his high throne because he was going to attack the Moors with valor; but cruel, thieving Death fearlessly robbed him, for it pardons no one, and killed him in Toledo.

121. He did a famous deed in his youth while you were in the city of Segovia of this state: he ordered that the noble inheritor, don Fernando, his brother, and the queen rule the kingdom after his death.

122. Noble King: you were well brought up by these noble rulers, nursed, and provided with very royal customs; for they were as loyal to you as it was well seen.

123. Your noble, dear mother and ruler, and the Infante went without delay to Guadalajara, since the king had ordered that they give you up to two grandees that he had named.

124. The kindling of your court and company burned, the town was quite disrupted and such a cruel and ugly struggle broke out, that if God had not soon intervened, it would have been like the multitude of Galea.

125. The noise was softened in such a way that the jealousies did not result in sin; so it was agreed that all should leave there, including yourself, and once they left, all would be quieted.

126. Then one morning you left with the queen for Valladolid in the plains, with many people that you brought along; and once they put you there, you did not go out to see the roads for ten years.

127. She kept you very carefully, more like gold than silver, like the cream of the milk; then your kingdom was equalled, for cruel death came with its poisonous arrow and killed her without her consent.

128. When the noble queen died, the people were saddened and disturbed by her death; however, as soon as she was buried, you rode through the town and examined your honorable court.

129. It was astutely ordered by all that the noble Juan Furtado be leader, and he said: "My Lord, leave this town and you will se your kingdom, and you will rest in the town of Madrid."

130. Then your court arrived in that town, along with great men whose names I will not mention here, and there you were given charge of the kingdom, since you had reached the age of majority.

131. The loyal men who were then guarding you took you to Segovia with your servants, in order to avoid danger or accidents in some lands between the two cities.

132. The relatives that entered that town with you did not want to admit more *infanzones* to the center; so they sought to clash head on, for they were already half fighting because of their stubbornness.

133. At the inn of your great majordomo, Juan Furtado, which is at the top of the paved road, an elegant party was given for you, with famous and great guests, but those on the outside and in the region paid a visit.

134. For they took them freely in their power and willingly took you from Segovia; those inside the city were made fools of, and blamed themselves, angered by the game.

135. At the inn mentioned above, the men inside bounced back with a trap; for one day later they attacked at Tordesillas, which was the evil and trouble of this new war.

136. For your royal house was entered, and that cavalcade burned much kindling; may God grant that it be extinguished without Castilla the Belabored suffering more ills.

137. Once this war was over, you, Sir, were taken within a few days, without dispute but not unwillingly, to the towered city, Avila the well protected, where you were indeed burdened.

138. For the Infantes separated into two groups, and showed banners of two distinct factions; one's men hid themselves on foot; the other's gathered many other people in Olmedo.

139. Since the problems were terrible and damaging, and since the two divisions were unfriendly between themselves, to avoid clashing they turned their backs to their adversaries and went to Talavera, carrying many flags.

140. You were safe with your noble family in that city with high walls; ... for one thing cares for the bay, while another attends him who saddles it.

141. He who notes that here is a good shot will rebound well in the game of ball and profit; the protectors did not know how to guard you well, for although they thought they did, something else happened at dawn.

142. Your loyal constable, who is very formidable with power and daring, loyalty and sentiment, and very beloved, with his coat of arms of Luna, arose early, alone, and did a very notable deed.

143. Sir, note what the loyal count did, since it is a deed which attests to greatness and loyalty: for to free you he cast you into a castle and guarded well the lock, fearing no one.

144. In Montalban is the tower in which you were, where, my Lord, you suffered great pain and anxiety; for lack of bread your loyal vassals fed you horsemeat, in spite of Saint Julian.

145. You were hidden there for nine days, in which those outside on barren land suffered great torment and were aggravated by bad weather, for the rains and the cold caused the river to swell so much that they could not find a ford.

146. Those inside suffered 100,000 shivers there, since for you they risked death and its terrors; their resentment for undergoing such adversity did not fade, like that of a deep lake with sighs and sweating.

147. Without further delay, those outside left and those inside took you healthy and free and without worry; for from then on they should consider that you were freed and ready to rule like a king.

148. Soon you rested with your people and you ruled, and after you left there you ruled your kingdom; you ordered and condemned, like a king and great lord, of some you had exiled.

149. You even made equal the great and the small, the poor and the rich, for you pardoned them all; for which, my Lord, you omitted from the kingdom all discrimination and you ordered it announced in markets and plazas.

150. Since everyone has seen other deeds that have been done in your kingdom, I shall not go on telling of them; for they would all be very disagreeable to repeat, and I believe that they are not even written in many texts and glosses.

151. So returning to the purpose mentioned above, which I write in verse, it is very fitting in its points; and so continue listening to what I say and propose, without fallacy or diphthong, rhyming my words.

152. If my above words are well considered, they will find that they are very well stated; for taking from you the victory of the good deed you began, your pleasure and glory were quite disturbed.

153. For you ordered that war be waged on the Moors, since you had enough money for what you decided; but as soon as you began to put it to work, you experienced as much trouble as the king whom you heard about.

154. A dishonest deed is known by all your grandees, and they know it in Flanders: that the daring kings entered, with valient gesture and with their outstretched banners, in Castilla, but with reserve.

155. They quickly arrived near Hita, but their stay was short and they returned without contention; that is why this deed seems a deep abyss to me, for I do not know who would inderstand such a dueling game.

156. You followed them entering into their kingdoms, destroying and burning as much as you could; but later, using your greatness, you did not consent to their doing more cruel deeds, and you were content.

157. If you look well at this burning, cruel, glowing fire, you will find that today you are in such necessities as was the king that I describe to you, and for more advice you should hear this.

158. For King Alfonso of Aragon and Sicily should have great compassion for his imprisoned and dead subjects; seeing his lands destroyed he will not have great patience, no more than seeing Valencia chased to its doors.

159. So, my Lord, think about don Juan, King of Navarra; it is seen that his land is singed very quickly; anyone can think about his sorrow and grief, for having such pain, he will have great torment.

160. So, Sir, whoever respects the Infantes that suffer, however rich they are, for Fortune destroys them; they are chased to the slaughter within Alburquerque, and the fire of olive oil is bad if it does not kill.

161. So, my Lord, your sister, the *Infanta,* is insecure, without pleasure or rest, sighing very listlessly because she is not as near you, King, as she was accustomed; so she sought the favor of her grandson of Santana.

162. So, Sir, Portugal is two-faced, for it discredits the logical sophism of the young men; the *Infante* don Duarte rocks the wagon, and he is not loyal to you.

163. And, my Lord, the enemies, those unloyal, Moorish dogs, that have wronged you a thousand times, will never be your friends; moreover, it is proven by experience, without witnesses, that they are a great plague and very contrary to this kingdom.

164. For, Sir, in the mountains of Castilla and its outskirts, he who tills the soil and he who plants discord does not die, for many play skillfully; this is what burns the most: to each his own way of reaping with his knife.

165. So, my Lord, open your eyes, for you should not sleep, but rather, soon provide by pulling out these thistles; if not, fields and stubbles will be plowed with lances and irrigated with blood, death, and spoils.

166. For, Sir, if this fire is not extinguished with a lot of water, before the flames burn more and the wound harms even more, this plague will be more terrible than the one France suffers, for its entire kingdom is destroyed by war and distance.

167. So therefore, help these evils with remedies, since you have so many means and needs, Sir, that they will cure so many corruptions of the mortal vipers and scorpions.

168. Oh brave, golden King of great honor, you are a generous, illustrious, eminent King; and the wise men find that this is the noblest kind that every monk and literate very much appreciates.

169. The precious and gentle Infanta is the noble, sovereign queen, who is so discrete and beautiful that her royal countenance and her gracious look are enough to cure this ill.

170. The narrow lancet is raised by the angel, your son, and he has kept it well; he will use that lancet and draw royal blood, because he will make Castilla happy without war.

171. The consoling *almina* which is opening the throat is your ruling sister, the good, saintly queen; it is a good idea to be with the lovely Infanta who shines like a star.

172. The advantageous plasters are the great gentlemen and loyal advisors who are very intelligent; they should be diligent for your service and God's, so that these dangerous deeds not take a turn for the worse.

173. The other plasters are the pastors and prelates of the Church, for they know the situation and your followers well; and if you persist with anger, may the wise doctors whom you trust so much read the historians well.

174. The very religious have under lock and key the olorous and bland balms; and they ask with many tears, fasts, and prayers that God punish this criminal deed.

175. The food and diets will not be only garbanzos, nor capons, nor wild duck, nor widgeon, but rather, very discrete persons, noble embassadors, loyal mediators, and men wiser than prophets.

176. The sweet, warm water in which they bathe the patient will not be brandy nor rose water; it will be the water from tears of lamentations and of the poor, for the land is destroyed by strong pursuit.

177. The comforting sugar will not be of roses nor violets, nor of bread, however delicious; but it will be more glorious than peace and concord, and once the discord is removed, the whole kingdom will rejoice.

178. The great, prudent doctor who must give the necessary comfort is only in Heaven on His excellent throne; and if He applies the balm with His blessed hands, the sick, with his distemper, is freed immediately.

179. It would be wise to seek a very good pharmacist in Castilla, to search for one who is very loyal and true; because of the sick one's welfare, the living, curing and dying depend on the herbolist.

180. For, my Lord, the medicines are strained through his sieve and with his hand he warms and stirs them; but they must avoid that his pot be of oleander wood, for if it is of olive wood, then many are also given the mallet.

181. For this reason, such an official should be very concerned and clearer than crystal, if he should take charge of the deed; and since the syrup is moderate and not bitter, Sir, may your loyal favorite take this charge.

182. For he is noble and powerful, astute and valient, courteous and serious, but above all, fortunate; for these reasons he deserves, and to him alone belongs, so important a task.

183. He carried out six famous and advantageous deeds, which were so loyal and well-known that they should be rewarded and praised by you, my King; these deeds, Sir, will be made known by me below.

184. The first deed: this person guarded you with great love and risked his life for you many times. The second is the great crown, which gave you much fame, for he guarded the royal bed from women.

185. The third: without malice, he guarded the sword from you, and he took from you the envy of having it bloodied. The fourth: because of him, your pen was guarded without deceptions, for you never wrote anything to harm yourself.

186. The fifth is the dignity that he guarded and you used, for you never disinherited anyone for mischief. The sixth is the prudence he kept well, for, Sir, you did not give up your fortresses easily.

187. For such great loyalty which he kept so well, he is and was quite worthy of remaining in your favor; and he should even have the guarantee of gradually acquiring better status, for he did no wrong to you.

188. For so long he knew great temperance, and he kept the weight just, as well as the balance; in joining peace and friendship, in mixing this syrup, he will have such judgement.

189. Eminent King: it is not necessary to praise his nobility, his astuteness and gentility, since the whole kingdom knows them well; and although I do not praise him, his own deeds do, and the nobles do not stop praising all his virtue.

190. Your palace produces many wise men who boast of love and are of great lineage; if they want to rid themselves of bad reputation, of falling to evil tongues, and of flying with rich wings, they should not read this slowly.

191. Step by step, I review briefly each of these deeds, for, my Lord, eminent, frank King, I want to get my point across, since I am nearing the end and concluding my writing.

192. I have recounted the life of the good king and the correction he wisely sought; for without lance nor shield, but only with his brain and doctrine did he give health and medicine to his kingdom.

193. Your Majesty should give this aid soon, giving remedies as needed to the suffering, and without complication, before it beats the devil with its stick; for his sting badly burns the one who sleeps soundly.

194. So that you understand my sermon, which is ending, it would be well that you listen soon and quickly; you know what the saintly and blessed King Alfonso did, and you will rejoice for that deed.

195. For your grandfather joined your father with the queen, your mother, and put him under cover, in order to cure the great fear that the Duke of Lancaster would easily win this kingdom.

196. Here is the solution for ridding of the bitterness and joining forever those peaces without any objection: may the entire kingdom beg you that your son, don Enrique, give great gifts to the flower (Infanta) of the Navarrese.

197. Then the humor and phlegm will be rid of, and the kingdom will be cleared of blood and tumor; and the net that is armed with the knots of the devil will be rid of without arms or arrows.

198. Then the sufferer will surely be healthy, and the Castilian King vibrant in great rest; therefore, Sir, help as soon as you can and do what you should, like a royal, Christian king.

199. And may a definitive, consoling judgement be spoken to you, which will be praised and written in letters of gold, in order to rid of the sadness and lamentation.

200. You will nobly pardon the kings, and using your royalty, reveal the Infantes; you will not kill other grandees; you will forget the errors of other, lesser men, giving them something with sincerity.

201. For their father (Fernando I of Aragon) did good services, which were praised and filled with loyalty; for he destroyed the Moors and their evil arrows, and in order to please you, he widened your kingdom.

202. On the border he obtained for you your lands, Santa Pligo, and the caves, and Cañete and Aznalmera; and he raised your banner in the tower of the caliph, and won from King Ozmin the towns of Xebar, Huete, and Antequera.

203. Contemplating your uncle, the noble king, who won so many people from the Moors by his sword, it seems that the sons of this family are worthy of pardon, for they do not ask more vengeance than noble blood.

204. The vengeance already taken is quite enough, for their land is completely destroyed; and, my Lord, it is also wasted by your great group of men; but spilled water is badly collected with a basket. (You can't regain what you have lost.)

205. Therefore, may your great anger cease and become gentle, so that the devil may not command more; for, Sir, if God wanted to give tranquility and peace, concord and solitude, this alone should be your interest.

206. Although it is not for me to give them advice, Your Majesty knows all of this; for looking at the family tree from which you and they came, all the battles and damages of this struggle will end.

207. Soon the combats at sea and on land will end; the cruel war and great debate will end, as well as many claps of thunder, and also bows, inquiries, pacts and *calcofates.*

208. There will be an end to warships and galleys; crude struggles, fights, and dissentions will end; an end will come to problems from foreign kingdoms, and money-spending; hearts will rest.

209. There will be an end to the noble French captains, the Genoese, Britons, and Germans, and the plundering of these birds of prey, and the great ornaments of Milan and Jasojarnes.

210. There will be an end to the coming of flags from other nations, the surrending of prisoners and retribution; an end will come to foreign immigration; much nobility in Castilla will cease not being dead.

211. An end will come to the robbers and they will see much disquiet; an end will come to those who take advantage of disorder, as well as to the killers who fear your presence, and to the evil and suffering; but sinners will live.

212. Soon money problems will end, along with borrowing and bribery; other affronts will end and happy people will rest; the towns and noblemen's lands will stay tranquil; many forced entries through our roads will end.

213. Carts will stop moving through the streets; the evils of arrows will stop the greedy; the prophecies of Merlin and Rocacelsa will cease to be; in this way the tambors and trumpets will also cease to sound.

214. There will be and end to traitors who weave false fabric, to fire, candles, and evil hunters, to troublemakers, false and disloyal men, to all evils, in spite of other troublemakers.

215. All the lamentations of the poor and suffering will end, as well as their great moans, crying and losses; and soon the lamentation of all who suffer will cease, as will all those who deserve to fear you.

216. The persecution and sighs of the people will end; they will stop cursing between their teeth; their tribulations will end, and they will pray for your life; the Church and its pardons will cease being chased.

217. There will be an end to the Portuguese and their whitlow, as well as to the Navarrese, the English, the Aragonese and all the little men; for the Moors there will be evil years and black months.

218. I ask of you, with the Virgin Mary, that your great sovereignty end all this fire and that it be done soon, before the summer begins; and if not, I wash my hands of it and withdraw them from the situation.

219. My art, written on parchment, has been done so you may live happily, without uprisings, for a long time; and, my Lord, I take God as my witness to what I say, for I am concerned for your welfare and I declare a good road ahead of you.

220. This is the end of my discourse; may God in Heaven keep you, care for you, and sustain you, and may Your Majesty consider my poem as a service to you.

Index of Names in the "Dezir"